YOU ARE THE KEY
Meera Jhogasundram

Jhogasundram debuts with a compact, inviting treatise on purposeful living crafted to introduce readers to self-awareness, self-acceptance, the practice of gratitude, and other avenues toward fulfillment. "You are the magician who can make your wishes come true," she writes, urging readers to stop making excuses–like being too old to start over–that might interfere with accomplishing their true desires. Emphasizing unconditional self-acceptance and the need for individuality, Jhogasundram offers some basic steps to overcome negative thoughts and boost intuition to successfully pursue your "heart's calling." Above all, she encourages readers to forgive themselves for past mistakes and learn how to believe in their own unlimited potential.

According to Jhogasundram, too many lives are spent trying to make others happy and conforming to unrealistic expectations. Instead, she teaches readers to reframe their anxieties and disappointments by understanding they can only control their own reactions to external events–and after they have done their best in any situation, the last recourse is to believe the Universe (her flexible term for a greater power) will bring their desires to fruition. Jhogasundram suggests that readers practice setting healthy boundaries to free up energy for pursuing their own interests, advising "you teach people how to treat you by the way you treat yourself."

YOU ARE THE KEY

7 Powerful Ways To Unlock The Life You Desire

MEERA JHOGASUNDRAM

For more information, email meera@meerajhogasundram.co.uk

ISBN: 978-2-9701533-0-6 (Print)
ISBN: 978-2-9701533-0-0 (Ebook)

*For my father, Jhogasundram and my mother, Jegajothy...
with love and gratitude.
You are my inspiration, my strength and my blessing!*

Your Free Gift

Thank you for purchasing my book!
I value each and every one of my readers.
As a gesture of gratitude, I'm offering a free digital product exclusively
for you, my readers.

"How to deal with toxic people – 3 effective ways!!!"

To learn more, go to the link below and get immediate access:

https://www.subscribepage.com/youarethekey

Table of contents

PHOTO BY: MEERA JHOGASUNDRAM

Author Note

Congratulations on taking this step to live a motivated and empowered life. Before you unlock this door, here are a few things to keep in mind. Some examples may resonate with you now. Others may resonate with you at a later stage. It's up to you to sieve what applies to your present situation and what you would like to work on. Prioritise your actions in your strategy to live your best life. You are at a unique point in your life and your journey is unique to you. My experiences and suggestions are intended to guide you back to your authentic self.

You will have experiences of your own. Through them, you will learn lessons meant for your growth. My book is meant to increase your consciousness in how you choose to live your life on a daily basis. If you are lost, there are guidelines to follow. If you have figured it out, what you read will empower you to do even better for yourself.

Your life experience begins with you. While you rarely have control over external circumstances, it is your choice to maintain the health of your inner being. While travelling through each page of my book, you will be inspired to take positive action so that you always aspire to be your best self, come what may. You have to be fine, well and happy before you can make a positive difference in the lives of those who matter to you. Doing your inner work is a priority. It is a necessity, not a luxury.

You are far more powerful than you think you are. It is important to cultivate the patience and perseverance required to wield your power.

There is no quick fix for living life to the fullest. The only way to achieve this is to live through your experiences gracefully and positively. Learn your lessons so well that you don't have to repeat them. Have faith in yourself and the power that created you.

You and I have begun this journey through this book. As the journey continues with my forthcoming books, you and I will evolve into better versions of ourselves. There is no end to personal growth. There will always be something that we can improve on, without comparing ourselves to others.

Be open and receptive to the messages embedded in my book. Choose not to criticise or judge yourself. Above all, choose not to give up. Believe in yourself. I believe in you!

Till we meet again...

Introduction

WHAT APPEARS TO BE A CHALLENGE IS ACTUALLY A BLESSING IN DISGUISE TO PREPARE YOU FOR RECEIVING A CONTINUOUS FLOW OF ABUNDANCE. – MEERA JHOGASUNDRAM

There have been many times in my journey when I've felt stuck. For instance, I didn't like the work situation I was in, but I loved my job. You must have had such conflicting feelings too. Maybe you still do. I believed for a long time that I wasn't capable of doing anything for a living besides the current job I had. I believed that I had no other skills. I believed that it was too late for me to learn new skills and eventually master them. I believed that my work situation would improve and that I would one day climb the corporate ladder. I believed that I was meant to be confined to my cubicle when I wasn't away from it carrying out my duties.

I believed that if I volunteered to take charge and participate in organisational activities, my contribution and talent would be recognised and rewarded. I believed that if I attended courses at my own expense, my commitment to professionalism would be appreciated and commended. I believed that the only way to career advancement was to upgrade myself from diploma to a bachelor's degree. When nothing changed, I believed that a master's degree would make a difference. Still nothing changed. After more than twenty years of dedicating my life and my attention to a job that I believed I loved, I found myself in the exact same position in the organisational hierarchy as when I first started work.

I don't wish for anyone to experience what I'm about to describe, but I know that many of you are in similar situations and continue to choose status quo because you believe that you have no choice. Well, that is actually a choice in itself. That is what you choose to believe! I don't mean to criticise or admonish you for the choices you've made so far. I'm here to tell you that you deserve better! I'm here to show you how you can do better!

What gives me the authority? I've been fighting this for a long time. What gives me the credibility? I've made choices that were not the best for me because of my self-limiting beliefs. Why should you listen to my advice? Because I want you to save precious time and reach your highest potential. Because I want you to give yourself a fair chance in life. Because I want you to believe in yourself enough to make changes in your life that may at first seem scary. Because I want you to know that you are worthy of the life you desire. Before that, I want you to believe that you are worthy!

How do I know that you are worthy when I don't even know you? The desire within you has surfaced for a reason. I want you to give that reason a chance. If you don't deserve to have that desire, it would not have been born within you. There is a reason for the dissatisfaction you're feeling. It's simply because you know you deserve more. For some reason, you're not acting on your discontentment. I'm here to show you why you should act without delay, without doubting yourself.

My dear friend, life is limited. Postponing your heart's calling is the best way to sabotage yourself. You're given a chance to experience all that our beautiful planet has to offer. You're given a chance to experience the wonder of our five senses. You're given a chance to explore your highest potential. You're given a chance to make wise choices – choices that are best for you. You're given a chance to live your dream. So, are you going to make use of this golden opportunity called *life* to be absolutely honest with yourself? Are you going to give your desires a fair chance? Or are you going to live up to others' expectations? What about your expectations? Have you mistaken your expectations for what is expected of you by society and those near and dear to you?

I'm here to show you why living a lie is a one-way road to disaster. The sooner you break free from façade in the form of society, the sooner you can begin living your life to the fullest. Age is no excuse. It's never too late to begin again. I know you must be sceptical reading that line because you've heard it being spoken far too often. Read it again. This time, believe it and know it. It's never too late to start anew! Self-limiting beliefs are not born with you. They are imposed on you from a very young age. You grow up believing that a particular achievement is the definition of success. You grow up believing that a particular status is the definition of happiness.

Somewhere down the road in your journey, you will realise that you've lost your identity, your true calling. You'll realise that your silenced desires and suppressed potential are screaming to be heard. You'll find yourself suffocating in what appears to be the ideal environment to thrive according to society's façade. You may argue that you've no clue what your calling is. Well, I'm here to show you that you can only discover the purpose of your life if you are true to yourself in your beliefs, thoughts, and actions. If you believe that you can do it and society tells you that you shouldn't, challenge it! If you believe that something is the best for you and you're told that it's beyond your reach, challenge it! Your life is far too short and precious to live according to the wishes of others. Only you know what you truly desire. Though you may have fears and doubts, only you know what you're truly capable of. Don't fall into society's trap and remain stuck for the rest of your life. Please honour yourself! Believe in yourself. Live life your way. Live your best life. Get unstuck! When you turn the pages, you'll discover simple ways to free yourself. You'll be inspired to do things that you've always wanted to do but never actually did. You'll learn why you are the star in your life.

There is so much within you that you haven't explored yet. Maybe you don't even know what's within you. What do I mean by that? Let me explain. Do you know what you're capable of? This is very different from what you think you're capable of within the scope of whatever you're doing right now. Have you tried something that triggered a desire, but before giving it a fair shot, you killed it with your ego, telling yourself

1. I'm too old for that, I should've started that when I was much younger. It's too late now.
2. I don't think I have the skills. I'm not good enough.
3. That's not for people like me.
4. I don't know if that's going to be of any use because I need to pay my bills.

5. What will people say? They're going to look down on me because I don't have a stable job.
6. It's nice to have that as a hobby but I'd rather make some extra money by working overtime; hobbies are not practical.

And the list goes on…

These are nothing but a bunch of self-limiting beliefs imposed on you from a very young age. You don't even realise that these beliefs are separate from who you truly are. You've no clue that you're sabotaging yourself.

I don't mean to find fault with your parents or your relatives or your upbringing. I'm calling you out for the lies you've been telling yourself for so long. How would anyone know your true desires, your true talents, and your true potential if you've been doing an excellent job at killing them all the moment they're born? You have to give yourself a chance. You owe it yourself. If you've always wanted to enrol in that photography class, do it! If you've always wanted to bake cakes, start baking! If you've always loved to sit by the lake alone, listening to nature and writing poetry, do it!

All I'm saying is that without giving yourself a chance to fulfil your desires, you'll never know what you're capable of. Of course, you have to earn a living and attain financial freedom. Of course, you want to live a comfortable life, especially in your later years. I'm not asking you to be irresponsible and not plan for the future. I'm telling you not to sacrifice living in the moment. How else can you experience life to the fullest without letting it pass you by?

There is a reason and purpose for the desires arising within you. It's your responsibility to discover what that is. It could turn out be just a hobby that gives you satisfaction or it could turn out to be related to your life purpose through which you give back to humanity and our planet. How do you expect to know your true purpose if you don't give yourself a chance?

Easier said than done, I know. You have commitments to fulfil. You have expectations to fulfil. I'm talking about what others expect from you. You have a reputation status to maintain. You want to be respected. You want success. What I'm going to help you see is that you've mapped society's definition of success onto what success means for you. Trust me, they are two entirely different things.

When you take some time out, distance yourself from the chatter in your mind, isolate yourself from the chatter around you and spend some time in nature by yourself, you'll know exactly what I'm talking about. You have to figure out your true path by yourself. That's a tough one! I've been there. I'm here to tell you that you can do it if you just give yourself a fair chance – no judgements, no scepticism, no criticism, no fears, no doubts.

You have to acknowledge your true desires without any external influence. I know you know what I'm talking about. Then you can work out how you're going to chase your dream and what kind of life you actually want to live. That life that you wish for yourself, not the life that you're expected to live. Then you can find ways to sustain yourself, living your dream. This may sound idealistic to you right now, but when you've had a taste of being absolutely honest with yourself, when you've had a taste of the freedom that such honesty brings, your choices for the future will become obvious.

You can be smart and responsible when you live life your way. You will live life to the fullest when you do what's best for you. You will live your best life when you're true to yourself. I'm here to show you how. But first, you have to allow me to help you. You have to be receptive to my suggestions. You must be willing to make some long overdue changes to your life. I believe you deserve to live at your highest potential.

Do you believe that you're deserving?

If your answer is yes, I invite you to turn the pages and read every word. I invite you to think about how you're going to implement the suggestions in ways that are most suited for you. I am so excited for you because you're going to discover things about yourself that you never knew until now. You're going to be triggered to move out of your comfort zone. You are going to start thinking about yourself first, fully understanding why you come first. Your perspectives and opinions will change. And it will be for the best. You may be uncomfortable in unfamiliar territory. You may have fears and doubts in the initial stages. That's perfectly normal. Work up your courage. Just continue being true to yourself. You'll never go wrong!

If your answer is no, then this book is clearly not for you. I suggest that you find something more suitable. And from the bottom of my heart, I wish you the very best in all your future endeavours!

Whatever your choice, know that I respect your decision. For those of you who've chosen to join me in this journey, I want to express my gratitude with the content in my book. I know that by reading it, you will be motivated to make at least one positive shift in your life. Often, that is all it takes. By sharing what I've learned from experience and through observation, I will make sure that you get unstuck! Each chapter builds into the next, so I strongly recommend that you avoid skipping chapters. You don't want to short-change yourself. I certainly don't want that for you. Travel this journey at your own pace. Don't rush. Instead, enjoy your adventure!

In my book, I refer to the power greater than us as the Universe. You can call it whatever you wish to, whatever it represents for you. What matters most is that you know there is a power greater than you, something that's responsible for creating you, something that will always lead you to your truth, something that will never let you down. I trust the Universe completely. I trust that you will trust the Universe completely!

*WHAT YOU SEE MAY BE **FAÇADE**. WHAT YOU THINK MAY BE **TRICKERY**. WHAT YOU FEEL MAY BE **MANIPULATION**. BUT WHAT YOU REALISE IS ALWAYS WHAT ACTUALLY IS. – MEERA JHOGASUNDRAM*

Chapter One

GET GROUNDED IN GRATITUDE

We take so many things in our life for granted. Sometimes we take people in our life for granted. So, when we experience loss, it feels like we are consumed by misfortune and there is nothing worth living for. When you're at what seems to be like the lowest ebb, have you ever asked yourself, Why am I still alive? A deep and profound question related to your life purpose. The answer to this will take you on a journey to self-discovery. The fact that you're asking this question is proof that there is a lack of gratitude in your reality. You may counter me by claiming that you pray and thank the divine regularly. You may say that you're very thankful for the people around you.

What I've realised is that saying it has nothing to do with living it. What do I mean by this? Are you doing things in your everyday life to show appreciation for what you have and the people around you? When things don't work out the way you think they should, are you constantly reminding yourself of all the things that are going well for you? Are you reminding yourself often enough to be grateful for how far you've come in life? It doesn't matter what point in your journey you're at now. If you're reading this, it is an indication that there's room for improvement in practising gratitude. I believe that there is no end point to being grateful. There will always be something more that you can be grateful for. You can't possibly run out of gratitude.

I lost my father in a car accident when I was around twelve. For the longest time, I was overwhelmed by his absence. I was focused on what

I should have had and not what I've always had since birth. When I lost my mother many years later, I was a mature, independent adult. So I thought! I couldn't have been more wrong. Her passing was a wake-up call to so many different things in my life. She was always there for me when I needed her and even when I thought I didn't need her. I understood how emotionally dependent I was on her only after she was gone for good.

I was broken. My spirit was broken. I went on pilgrimages to offer prayers for both my parents so that their souls would rest in peace. I felt guilt. I felt grief. I felt that I was the most unfortunate soul on earth. I felt that life was unfair. I didn't see why I should appreciate anything anymore. I was angry. I wanted answers. I wanted to know why I had to endure such great losses in my life.

In 2014, I went on a pilgrimage to Kedarnath, an ancient temple on the top of a mountain in the greater Himalayan range. I planned the questions I wanted to ask God. I wanted to know why life was so unfair to me. I didn't know why I was still alive when all I had been experiencing was loss. I wanted answers. I demanded answers. Because as far as I was concerned, I've always been nothing but genuine and sincere. If you catch my drift, I was in a victim mindset and everything bad was happening to me.

During the challenging journey up the mountain, something interesting and enlightening happened. There was massive destruction in Kedarnath due to previous floods. Many people had lost their lives. I heard about this, but because I was the 'unfortunate' one, I didn't pay much attention to what was being said. I was consumed by grief, anger, and of course, self-pity. Because of the natural disaster, the path up Kedarnath was tricky and dangerous. We had to take each step very carefully on foot as the path was muddy, slippery, and extremely narrow. One wrong step and I would fall off the mountain. I remember thinking to myself, 'If that happened, I don't think anyone would be able to find me, definitely not in such terrain.'

Here comes the interesting part. Remember, I didn't know why I was still alive. I didn't see the point of my existence. Yet, I was frantically chanting my prayers for each step that I took because I was afraid of falling off. Why? Because I didn't want to die. Aha! That's when I felt shamed by my own hypocrisy. I didn't see a point in living, and at the same time, I was terrified of dying. I quickly concluded that yes, I wanted to live. Why? I didn't have all the answers at that point. I didn't need to know why. All I had to admit to myself was that I wanted to live!

It then struck me that I have so much to be grateful for, despite having lost my parents. Firstly, I was grateful that I survived the dangerous journey, especially during the times when I was on a pony and it was so easy to fall off, never to be found again. I was grateful for being alive. I was grateful that I reached the top of the mountain and made it back. I was grateful for every single thing in my life, everything that brought me to that point in life's journey.

One more thing – when I entered the temple, I didn't feel like asking any questions though I still didn't know the answers. I was just plain grateful for being alive. I don't know how, but I knew that I had a specific purpose. I knew that it would be revealed to me with time. I knew that everything has its own timing. I learned never to question the timing of the Universe. When it's time to go, we've got to go. So, when it's time to live, *we better live in gratitude!*

I want you to understand that this is a snippet of the countless moments of gratitude that I've experienced in my life. It is by no means the be-all and end-all. It was a beautiful moment of self-realisation, which is a process that we experience throughout our lives till our very last breath. So why did I pick this story to tell you? Because being alive is the most basic reason to be grateful for, but we continue to take it for granted. Be grateful that you're alive. Be grateful that you've been given a chance to experience life. Be grateful for every breath you take because there will come a day when it's time to stop. Till then, you owe it to yourself to *keep going forward!*

Why should you ground yourself in gratitude? Because being grateful prevents you from falling into the 'lack' trap. When you're grateful for everything that you have and everything that you are, there is no way you're going to feel deprived of something. That doesn't mean that you shouldn't aspire for more to be more. Of course, you should! The difference is the mindset of abundance that you will inevitably cultivate by practising gratitude. If you're reading this, I'm sure you've been exposed to negative thoughts and toxic environments. Gratitude is a quick remedy for such situations. When you're grateful, you're consciously focusing on the positive in your life. When you're grateful, you're living mindfully. You will have peace of mind. You will be in alignment with your goals and desires. You will be able to reach for your highest potential. Gratitude is the most basic, as well as the greatest, enabler in your life.

How do you practise gratitude daily and make it a way of life? What are the simple things you can do to make sure that you are living in gratitude? When you're crippled by fear, be grateful for coming this far in life, despite the choices you've made. When you're in doubt, be grateful that you've been given the chance to make a choice. Be grateful that you've been given the opportunity to exercise your free will. When your weakness overwhelms you, be grateful that you're being shown what's not meant for you and how much more you need to do to improve.

Be grateful for the air you breathe, the food you eat, the water you drink. Be grateful for your health. You get my drift! Nothing should be taken for granted. What if your basic needs are not fulfilled? Would you then be in a frame of mind to feel disappointed over not being able to afford the house you dreamed of living in? It's human to want more and to have dreams. All I'm saying is don't dismiss all that you already have. Many don't have even that!

This is what I mean when I say, 'live in gratitude.' When you're in a challenging situation at work or at home, be grateful for the chance to make whatever change is required. Remember, you always have a choice! Find the positive in every negative that you encounter. This is best done with gratitude. When things don't go your way, be grateful for the lesson. There is always something to be grateful for.

I don't believe in one specific way of practising gratitude. You could do it all day, every day. You could do it when you're walking on the street or on your way to the train station. You could do it while having your shower. However and whenever you choose to feel this powerful emotion is totally up to you. We are all unique beings. That's what makes each of us special. You decide what works best for you. You don't need to schedule a time to feel gratitude. You can do it whenever you like.

Having said that, I do realise that 'whenever you like' could easily become 'never.' So, I'm going to suggest something to get you started. Once you become a seasoned practitioner of gratitude, you will come up with what works best for you. Before you go to bed, just say 'thank you.' The first thing in the morning, when you open your eyes, say 'thank you.' You don't even have to say what or who you're thankful for. Just say the two words and mean it. If you're already practising gratitude, that's great! I'm so proud of you. But for those who just can't seem to get started in gratitude, do what I suggested and mean it when you say it. This may seem very basic and mundane to you. You'll be amazed at how you feel after a week of just doing this, nothing more.

You may want to list the things you're grateful for daily, but that could feel like a chore when all you want to do is go to bed. There will come a point when you have a desire to be explicit about the things you're grateful for. You'll know when. You'll know what to say. There will come a point when feeling gratitude becomes second nature. You'll be thankful for the rain. You'll be thankful for the sun. Need I say more! You may think that such practices are beyond you. Trust me on this. It will happen so spontaneously that you'll be surprised. This happens with time. Each person's journey is different, so please don't impose benchmarks and timeframes for something that's felt in your heart. Make an honest effort. Begin with something very simple so that you stick to it. Make sure you do it every day. You'll never go wrong!

Don't worry. I'm not going to leave you in a limbo with just 'thank you' in the first chapter. When you feel that you're ready for more, here are some suggestions. Feel free to use them. I would prefer that you change it according to your preference. Personalise it in whatever way you can.

1. I am so grateful that my basic needs are fulfilled.
2. I am so grateful that my health is improving.
3. I am so grateful that I am able to do things for myself.
4. I am so grateful that I realise the value of life.
5. I am so grateful for all the lessons I am learning and continuing to learn in my life.
6. I am so grateful for all the guidance I am receiving all the time, in different ways, through different people throughout my life.
7. I am so grateful that I have enough.
8. I am so grateful that I am enough.
9. I am so grateful for the moments in my life that make me smile.
10. I am so grateful that I love myself.
11. I am so grateful that I accept myself unconditionally.
12. I am so grateful for my strengths and weaknesses.
13. I am so grateful that I am able to find strength in my

weaknesses.

14. I am so grateful that I am motivated to live my dream.
15. I am so grateful that I am taking inspired action.
16. I am so grateful for the love in my life.
17. I am so grateful for my creativity.
18. I am so grateful that I am passionate about reaching my highest potential.
19. I am so grateful I have a mindset of abundance.
20. I am so grateful for the happiness, prosperity, and peace in my life.

Make a ritual out of your gratitude affirmations in a way that gives you the most satisfaction. Remind yourself of all the things, the little things and the big things, that you're grateful for as often as possible. When you feel insecure, doubtful, fearful or anxious, quickly remind yourself of something that you're grateful for. It's tough but not impossible. It's a conscious effort that you choose to make to live a more beautiful life. Are you going to do it? Look at it this way – you've absolutely nothing to lose and everything to gain. So why not?

My wish for you is to come up with your own set of affirmations unique to your situation. You must be so comfortable and familiar with it that it plays in your mind without you making a conscious effort to think about it. You will feel positive and happy when your unique affirmations become a natural way of living. Before you reach this stage, you will of course have to remind yourself regularly of all that you're grateful for. There will come a point when you feel off balance without your daily dose of gratitude. That's when you know that you have succeeded in living in gratitude. My request to you is to please go at your own pace. You have emotional burdens and negativity of the past, maybe present, exclusive to you. You decide how you'd like to incorporate your affirmations into your life, at what pace, and when you'd be comfortable making a routine out of them. You will have a clearer picture when you've confirmed what your special affirmations are going to be.

You may stop after a few days. Start again! You may not feel much difference after perhaps a week. Persevere! Your affirmations are not a magic spell to work instantly. You are learning to become a master manifestor. You are in the process of manifesting gratitude and abundance in your life. That takes time. Each person's process is different. You've got to trust your journey. You've got to trust the process. Most importantly, you've got to trust your intuition. How do you do this? Well, that's what Chapter Two is for. Without having gratitude, you won't be able to trust your intuition because you won't hear it. Why? Because ego will take the place of gratitude and will dictate your actions, whether or not you realise it – whether or not you admit it.

I'd like to close this chapter by telling you that I am extremely grateful for having the opportunity to make your life more meaningful, and I trust, more beautiful. I am grateful that you're reading my book. I am grateful that you're considering my humble suggestions. I am grateful that you're giving me your undivided attention, and thus, your precious time. I am grateful that you've completed this chapter successfully. I am grateful for your support. I am grateful that you're open and willing to improve your life. I am grateful for you!

BE GRATEFUL BECAUSE IT COULD HAVE BEEN WORSE. BE GRATEFUL BECAUSE YOU HAVE MADE IT TO THIS MOMENT. BE GRATEFUL BECAUSE IT WILL GET BETTER. – MEERA JHOGASUNDRAM

Chapter Two

Trust Your Intuition

I'm often asked these questions: How do you know that the voice you're hearing is your intuition and not your ego? How can you be sure? I know the answer too well because I learned it the hard way. Here's how I made the discovery. I started working at 21. I worked in an organisation for many years. I was very proud to work there. To me, the job was professional, and it gave lots of exposure to information that I would otherwise not be aware of. It built my confidence. It advanced my job skills. I thought I was happy because the nature of the job kept me on my feet, always motivating me to do better and upgrade myself.

Apparently, this is only one aspect of job satisfaction. I learned the hard way that my immediate work environment was one of the most important factors determining how far I progressed in my career and how peacefully I did it. Unfortunately for me, my workspace was filled with toxicity and backstabbing. Clique systems thrived. People got together to bring down the few who refused to give up their individuality for the sake of being accepted in groups. These groups consisted of people whose main goal in life was to gossip and conspire. This was my immediate work environment. Fortunately, it had nothing to do with the organisation I was working for. I was at the bottom of the organisational hierarchy, and mine was a ground-level job. While I was proud to be part of the organisation, from day one, my intuition kept telling me that my immediate work environment was ill-suited for me.

I ignored it. I told myself that if I persisted in being patient and focused on upgrading myself, my efforts would be acknowledged. I would be given due recognition. I worked so hard to divert and minimise the negativity aimed at me. I was judged for being an introvert. I was judged for choosing not to be part of any clique. I was judged for upgrading my academic qualifications. I was judged for speaking my truth and speaking my mind. I was judged for aspiring to advance in my career. I was fully aware that I was being judged. My intuition kept prompting me and cautioning me. Still, I told myself that I was not a victim and I had things under control. I believed that apart from that job, there was nothing else that I could excel in. I believed that I would somehow get a transfer to another department based on my qualifications.

You'll be surprised at how long I postponed trusting my intuition and acting on it. I completed my diploma. I got my bachelor's degree. I did my master's. And guess what? The situation at work became worse. My hope for the ideal change remained unrealised. My aspirations for career advancement were destroyed. After more than 22 years of dedicating my precious life to a job that I respect so much and will always respect, I found myself at the same position in the organisational hierarchy. Can you imagine how I felt? More than two decades is too long a time to hope for a change. I learned it the hard way. It was not only the hope; a lot of my unpleasant experience had to do with my self-limiting beliefs.

That's when it hit me. My intuition had been warning me every step of the way. It was desperately trying to guide me. I chose not to heed its advice. My intuition had been eagerly trying to steer me in a direction that was truly meant for me. I chose to turn a blind eye. My intuition was constantly telling me to leave the job. I refused to listen. Instead, I chose to rely on my ego, which succeeded in making me believe that I was capable of doing only that job, I had no other option that would make me happy, I was too old to make a career switch, and it was best to stick to that job because it gave me financial security. I chose to nurture the false belief that things would change for the better. Well, nothing changed. Situations worsened! This is my experience and my perspective. There were others who thrived and got their promotions and advanced their careers. It was the place for them. Not for me. Precisely what my intuition tried to tell me for so long, but I kept silencing it.

I paid a very high price. I spent a large part of my life living painful experiences because I didn't trust my inner guidance. I suppressed its voice. I never gave it a chance. The best part – I didn't even realise that I was doing these things. It was mostly done on a subconscious level. I was so blinded by my ego and self-limiting beliefs that I couldn't see life passing me by. I was so focused on superficial expectations imposed on me by society that I never gave my true desires a chance to flourish. I take full responsibility for this huge mistake. I was the one who chose to fit in with external expectations. This turned out to be an undesirable choice, a lesson well learned!

In fact, I always had a choice. I should have left that job after five years at the most. I didn't. I could have spent my time focusing on what I truly wanted to do for the rest of my life. Instead, I was busy doing what was expected of me. These heavily compromised choices are a direct consequence of not trusting my intuition. Having said that, I must admit that it can be quite intimidating to follow your inner guidance. Why? Because it will push you out of your comfort zone. It will stretch your potential to its limit. It will compel you to follow your heart's desire when it seems impractical or even impossible to you. Your intuition will bring out the best in you. Mine did. You will discover numerous possibilities due to your broadened perception. You will realise that you're capable of so much more than you had ever imagined. You will be enlightened on what your true path is. Your inner voice will keep propelling you forward. If you don't, you'll end up feeling uneasy and frustrated. There will always be a yearning in your heart, calling you out for not doing what you know you're meant to do.

This may seem too deep for some of you. It may make you feel uncomfortable. Perhaps you never gave yourself a chance in certain things. Perhaps you never gave your true desires a chance. My humble request to you – don't let life pass you by. Your time on this beautiful planet is limited. Yes, you do learn from mistakes. But you'll have more time to do what you're called upon to do by your inner guide if you're also willing to learn from mistakes made by others. I always make sure that I give a positive spin to whatever happens in my life. Looking back, I would say that I've learned numerous lessons and I've become much wiser after more than two decades of bad judgement coupled with complacency. I have a wealth of experience. At the same time, I'm acutely aware that I could have made far better choices. I could have believed in myself and in my abilities more. I don't dwell on these, but

I remember the lessons. Why? I'm going to make sure that I make the best choices for myself based on what I've learned. I discovered what's best for me. I acted on it. Here I am, telling you my story.

Let me make it easier for you. Always give a positive spin to occurrences in your life. Up to this point, if you've not been trusting and following your inner guidance, it's alright! No one is perfect. Henceforth, you've no excuse. You cannot 'not know' what you've just read. You can no longer ignore the voice within you. If you try to, it's going to become more and more challenging. And I'm so glad for being the instrument causing a shift within you. The positive change within you is long overdue.

Whether or not you've been following your inner guidance, there's always room for improvement. If you've never heard your inner voice, silence your mind and listen up. If you've not trusted your inner guide, start trusting. If you've been following your intuition, do it more frequently. Make it a way of life. The more you rely on it, the stronger it becomes, just like a muscle. It's always looking out for you. It's always working for you. It's always working with you. It's your best friend. It's your best guide.

So how do you make sure that you trust your intuition? Let's get down to the juicy details.

1. FEEL MORE

Never rush into making any decision. You will have an initial feeling about a certain situation. It may very well be your intuition helping you. It could also be your personal preferences or bias. It could be your self-limiting beliefs. It could be your judgemental nature. It could be myriad possibilities. How can you tell for sure that it's your intuition? By giving yourself some time to come to a conclusion, without input from others, without the influence of your preconceived ideas. You've got to do this by yourself. Take some time out by yourself, with yourself. For instance, go to your favourite spot at home or somewhere in nature. Relax yourself. Silence your mind's chatter. Take in the warmth and comfort of your environment. Think less. Feel more! How does your body react when you recall the specific situation? Do you feel at ease or do you become anxious?

2. GIVE IT TIME

At this point, you're ready to hear your inner voice. Listen to it without doubting it or questioning it. You may not like the response from your inner guide. You may not agree. You may feel uncomfortable, uncertain, even fearful of what could happen if you were to trust your intuition and act on it. Therein lies the challenge. It requires courage, determination and perseverance to follow through with your inner guidance. No matter how difficult you think it may be, never ignore that voice. You may believe that you have neither the courage nor the willpower to do what you've been guided to do. It's a natural feeling. Just don't decide on anything when you feel this way. Don't act against your gut instinct. Give it some time.

Keep an open mind. Let nature take its course. Let the Universe show you the way. This may sound weird and beyond your present reality. Still, give it time. As events unfold before your eyes, as you receive signs and signals in your daily life, you will realise and understand that your intuition was right all along.

3. BE WARY OF EXTERNAL ADVICE

Before seeking advice from anyone, believe in yourself enough to trust your intuition. I'm not claiming that external advice is pointless. I'm merely stressing the need for you to rely on yourself first. Why? Those you intend to approach for guidance have their own set of bias and prejudice. They have their own set of self-limiting beliefs based on their unique life experiences. They may not even be aware that their beliefs are self-limiting. Their reality is not your reality. This is crucial for you to grasp. You're in a vulnerable state. You're not sure what to do. You're confused. You certainly don't want to succumb to the wrong advice. Though you may not have all the answers, time will guide you. Time will give you clues. Be receptive to your own guidance. That is the best guidance for you.

4. DO IT YOUR WAY

You've given yourself some time. You've built up the courage to take action. But you're not sure exactly how to do it. You want to know the best approach. By all means, seek guidance from those who've gone through similar challenges. Learn from their experiences. Sieve what's relevant to your situation. Leave out the rest. Even here, your intuition will kick in. Be discerning. Make sure no opinions are imposed on you. You will be the one to decide exactly what to do and how to do it, after considering all possible options. Do what's most suitable for you. When you do it your way, trusting your intuition, it's a sign that you're on the path that's best for you.

5. NURTURE YOUR INNER CHILD

There is a way to make sure that you're constantly in touch with your intuition. Pay attention to the needs and wants of your inner child. That is who you are in your element. Your inner child never lies. They are the essence of your life experiences. What do I mean by that? You feel emotions through your inner child. You connect with those who matter most to you through your inner child. You connect with nature through your inner child. Your creativity is sparked by your inner child. You learn how to laugh and play through your inner child. I'm no expert to tell you the link between your intuition and your inner child. But I can say this for sure…both are within you. Both depend on you to thrive. Both can become your greatest strength if you allow it.

How do you nurture your inner child?

- When you feel like having an ice cream in the depth of winter, do it!
- When you feel like dipping your feet in the lake, do it!
- When you feel like singing your favourite song while walking on the street, do it! (Just don't cause any public alarm.)
- When you feel like sitting on the grass and listening to the birds conversing, do it!
- When you feel like watching the movies that you watched as a child, do it!
- When you feel like getting drenched in the rain, do it! (This one is my personal favourite!)
- When you feel like dancing in the shower, do it!
- If you love animals and love feeding them, make sure you

do it! (This is top on my list!) Spend time with them. They get you the way no one else does. They connect with your inner child instantly.

- Spend time in nature. You're made up of nature's elements. You just can't help being your true self in nature.
- Catch up with childhood friends. Relive the good times you shared. No one had to teach you how to play when you were a kid. No one had to show you how to be joyful. No one had to train you to laugh. You did it all by yourself. You were being true to yourself. That's you in your natural state.

When your inner child is starved, you lose motivation. You won't feel like doing anything productive. You may find yourself staring into emptiness. You know that something is missing in your life. Your inner child is the essence of who you are. That's you in your element. That's you minus all the fluff. When your inner child thrives, you will thrive. When your inner child is nourished, your creativity will flourish. When your inner child is excited, you will be motivated. You'll be perked up and passionate about life. You'll get that spark back.

Look after your inner child – the one who's born with you, within you. The one who'll be with you till your last breath, the one who has the power to make you live life to the fullest!

6. TRUST YOUR JOURNEY

You've got to believe in yourself enough to trust your unique journey in life. Though this quality will be covered in detail in the next chapter, I have to touch on it here. Your intuition is your best guide on life's journey. The challenge is to have faith in your life path, though it may be drastically different from that of your peers. You can't afford to be fickle in pursuing your calling. It may not be in alignment with the values you grew up with. It may not be in sync with tradition. It may go against cultural norms and behaviour. Still, you've got to stick to what you can do best, what you want to do.

Don't even think about comparing yourself with anyone. Understand that the combination of your strengths, weaknesses, and life experiences make you beautifully unique. Own your uniqueness! When you achieve this, you'll spontaneously trust your intuition more. It could also work the other way. When you learn to trust your intuition more, you'll be led to your true worth. You'll understand that what's meant for you is unique to you. You'll know that your journey is yours to travel. You can't be stopping and waiting for company. Whoever is aligned with your goals and beliefs will join you at the right time.

So, which comes first – trusting your intuition or trusting your journey? That's up to you, my friend! In your life, you'll be the judge of that. A lot depends on how you choose to evolve into your highest potential. Of course, your intuition will be guiding you. You just have to make sure that you don't ignore anything that you feel in your gut.

TRUSTING YOUR INTUITION WOULD MEAN TRUSTING YOURSELF, TRUSTING YOUR JOURNEY, AND ABOVE ALL, TRUSTING YOUR LIFE PURPOSE. – MEERA JHOGASUNDRAM

Chapter Three

ACCEPT YOURSELF UNCONDITIONALLY

D o you accept the mistakes you've made? Have you forgiven yourself? Do you accept your weaknesses? Do you accept your inabilities? Perhaps a few of these may genuinely be your shortcomings. Most of these are usually in relation to what is expected of you by someone or some people. The next time you think less of yourself, make a conscious effort to interrupt that thought. Question it. Challenge it. Perfection is a myth. And if you insist on achieving perfection, know that you are a creation of perfect imperfection. Being the best in something is a momentary feeling. It will not last simply because there will always be someone better than you in some way. There will always be someone better than you at something.

Accept yourself the way you are, unconditionally. Then, you can choose how much more you wish to improve. Then, you can choose how to empower yourself. Then, you can choose the path of your growth. Bottom line – you have absolutely no excuse not to accept yourself without 'ifs' and 'buts'.

I've observed that it's a fashion statement to be part of a group, be it a cultural group, a work group, or a group of friends. The 'in' thing is to be included by the most popular and often the most vocal group in a social setting. I understand that this could start as early as your teen years. I must admit the clique system serves the insecurities of people desperate to fit in. They would go to great lengths to edit themselves in order to fit into a clique that cripples their creativity and stunts their individuality.

It's important to connect with people and achieve goals as a team, especially in a work environment. However, if this compromises your potential and ambition, it could cause you irreversible loss. How? You could lose precious time – time that you could have used to upgrade yourself; time that you could have used to explore your interests. If the group of people you're required to fit in with is toxic and low-vibrational, you're on the road to self-sabotage.

In my case, I made a conscious effort not to fit into any clique. That wasn't hard. I am an introvert. I am also outspoken, and I strongly believe in speaking my truth, especially against any injustice I encounter in the workplace. While there were other introverts in my immediate work environment, apart from us, the majority thrived on belonging and functioning in various cliques. All I had to do was be true to myself and I would naturally not fit in.

Gosh! It was challenging! I was judged and criticised for my interests. I was accused of being anti-social when it was actually my introverted nature at play. Because I was straightforward in my dealings, I became predictable, and it was easy to backstab me and push me into tricky situations. I learned that belonging to a group can give me power over someone who was 'alone'. But it is power that corrupts. This ideology was misaligned with my goals and aspirations. It went against my principles. I chose not to be a hypocrite.

I have to be honest. There were times when I felt miserable. There were times when I felt insulted and humiliated. Still, I never stopped believing in being true to myself. I didn't know how to live otherwise. I can't explain it, but I just couldn't live a lie. It was a very tough, trying, and long period. I hoped many times that things would change for the better, but it only became worse. I was discouraged and disappointed, and I felt disempowered. Still, I was proud of always being honest with myself and accepting myself unconditionally.

The Universe has its own magical way of rewarding you when you do your part. Things happened in a way that made me choose to leave that environment. Yes, it was my choice, and I have absolutely no regrets! All my experiences have made me strong and courageous. Most importantly, they prepared me for the most beautiful journey I have ever experienced in my life. A journey that empowered me to discover my true self, my purpose, and my dream. It was that journey that led me to write this book.

Bottom line – I would not be where I am now if I had not accepted myself unconditionally. Despite my inability to succeed in my career, despite not being accepted by the people around me, despite the criticism and judgement imposed on me, despite all the insults and humiliation, despite all the odds against me, I chose to accept myself for who I am. That's what matters most!

Though I tried to do things that I thought would please the people I had to work with, it was never enough. Though I did my best in carrying out my duties as a team member, it was never enough. I was certainly not prepared to compromise my authenticity and lose my individuality. I paid a high price for this – more than 20 years of stagnancy at the workplace. Now, from where I am, I can confidently say that it was all worth it. I'm making sure that every lesson has been learned perfectly well. No way am I making the same mistakes again!

This story is not meant to discourage you. My intention is to make you see the importance of accepting yourself without any conditions, even if no one else accepts you. You've got to be there for yourself. You've got to be proud of who you are. What you think about yourself matters more than what anyone else thinks about you. Of course, you would care about how your loved ones see you. That's natural. What I'm saying is, how you see yourself comes first!

How exactly can you go about accepting yourself without any conditions? Let me help you.

1. FORGIVE YOURSELF

First and foremost, forgive yourself for all that you think you would have done, should have done, and could have done. Forgive yourself for all that you could have done better. Forgive yourself for all that you should not have done (all that you should not have put up with).

However you choose to reflect on the past, if it makes you feel less of yourself, it's clearly not doing you any good. Forgive yourself for choosing to be in toxic situations for as long as you were. Remember, we always have a choice. The sooner we take responsibility for our not-so-wise choices, the sooner we can improve our lives.

Move forward. Keep your thoughts, feelings and actions on where you're heading, not where you came from. To do this, you must make sure that you have forgiven yourself completely. Forgiveness will give you a new lease of life. It's the first step to accepting yourself without any condition.

2. OWN YOUR UNIQUENESS

Believe, understand, and know that you are unique. Just to refresh your memory, I touched on this in the previous chapter. You're defined by your strengths as well as your weaknesses. The way in which you experience life is unique to you. The combination of your beliefs, thoughts, and feelings is unique to you. Your contribution to humanity and our planet is unique. There is only *one you*.

This being the case, any comparison would make no sense. If you must compare, please compare who you are now with who you were before. That way, you will not miss the challenges that you've overcome to reach this point of your journey. Don't trivialise your struggles. You'll naturally be grateful for coming this far in life, given your choices, despite your choices. Be proud of yourself. You are beautifully unique. Own it!

3. FIND STRENGTH IN WEAKNESSES

What you perceive to be your weakness, whatever that may be, know that the more you try to hide it, the more insecure you become. Look into the eyes of your shortcomings. Stare into the eyes of fear. Understand that it's perfectly alright to have limitations. Do the best you can do given your constraints. This way, you will not find any reason to criticise yourself or even blame yourself.

Be content and grateful that you're able to do that much. Be proud of yourself for choosing to do that much. Again, I'd like to reiterate the fact that you always have a choice. You could have easily chosen to do otherwise. Give yourself credit when it's due. This is how you find strength in what you perceive to be your weakness. I consider it to be your perception because I believe that it's up to you to turn into your strength. That's what this book is all about. You've got to realise that you're not as powerless as you believe you are.

Respect Yourself First

A crystal-clear sign that you've indeed accepted yourself without any condition is when you naturally begin respecting yourself first.

You must be thinking, 'Of course I respect myself! It's a no-brainer'. Really? Are you sure? Do you respect yourself enough or are you busy respecting others more than yourself? Do you actually respect yourself first? Or does someone or everyone come before you? Stop lying to yourself. Face it.

You better respect yourself more! You better respect yourself first! There are fundamental ways to make sure that you are doing this. I'm giving you three suggestions. Make full use of them. At the same time, remain true to your authentic self.

- When you have a thought or opinion, speak your truth. It may not be accepted. It may be shunned. It may even be mocked. Still, speak your truth! Why? Because what you think counts. Because you matter. Because your truth is worth listening to.
- When you feel that something is not right for you, honour your feelings. Express yourself. No justification needed. You are being *you*. You are being authentic. That's what matters. You have a right to feel the way you do. There's a reason for you to feel the way you do. You owe it to yourself to do what's best for you.
- When you have a dream, chase it. Easier said than done, I know. But you are worth it. There's a reason for your desire. Respect it. Give yourself the best gift of living your best life. You deserve it!

It's time to live your way, because in your life, *you come first*. Respect yourself first!

In this chapter, I've crafted self-respect as a subset of unconditional self-acceptance. I want to stress that it could work the other way. You may feel comfortable making it a point to do things to ensure that you come first. Go ahead! Do what's best for you in the order that works best for you. The purpose of this book is to trigger awareness and provoke positive action. My suggestions are not meant to dictate in an authoritarian fashion exactly how you ought to conduct your life. Take what suits your personality, character, and lifestyle. Personalise it. Keep shining throughout your life. That's my wish for you.

4. Know Your Worth

There will be times when situations or people trigger your insecurities. You may feel and think less of yourself. You may feel that you need to do more to be accepted. You may want to prove yourself and your worth. My question to you, Do you know your worth? If you are aware of your significance, you wouldn't feel the need to prove yourself to anyone. If someone doesn't realise your worth after you've given them ample opportunities, it's a clear sign from the Universe that they're not aligned with who you are. Trying to convince someone of your worth would mean that you're compromising it. Those who value you do not need any convincing.

You just have to aspire to be your best self all the time. There will be occasions when you fall short of your aspiration. Pick yourself up and move forward. You're human. You're entitled to make mistakes. Make sure you learn the lessons. When you're constantly working on how you can improve your life and better yourself mentally, emotionally and spiritually, you will realise your true worth.

Those who recognise your worth will naturally align themselves with you. How? Through mutual respect and admiration. Through friendship. Through common interests and goals. Through honesty and authenticity.

Don't attempt to edit yourself to fit into another person's requirements. This is a recipe for deep-rooted dissatisfaction over time. People should accept you for who you are, not who they want you to be. The sooner you realise this, the sooner you understand your worth.

5. Build Confidence from Within

Have you come across people who brag about themselves, their lifestyle, their vacations, their children, their social status, etc.? How does that make you feel? What impression do you get from their behaviour? What does your gut instinct tell you about them? That's right. At the very least, you get the impression that they're trying very hard to keep up with the Joneses. Simply put – they're compensating for their insecurities. They're probably trying to match up to something or fit into a social class, or they're simply trying to make themselves feel more important. We can't criticise them for choosing to behave this way. But we can make a quick mental note on what we shouldn't be doing if we're genuinely confident.

Such confidence on display is a façade. If you observe them, you'll find that they're seeking respect and admiration from those they're bragging to. This becomes completely unnecessary when you know your worth and you're confident from within. Why not respect yourself and admire yourself for all your achievements? This has nothing to do with being selfish and everything to do with self-love. I'll talk about loving yourself in detail later (Chapter Four).

Confidence from within brings about calmness. It is silent. It never brags. It never tries to prove its worth. When you've built such confidence, what others say and think about you will have minimal effect on your life. You will be able to disregard anything that's not in your best interest, anything that no longer serves you. You will be able to accept yourself easily.

If you haven't already figured it out, my how-to suggestions build into one another. The effect of the combination of these suggestions is far greater than any one of them practised on its own.

6. CALL OUT NEGATIVE THOUGHTS

You thought you had it under control. You were fine, happy and confident for some time. You were beginning to enjoy thinking and feeling positive. Everything was going great until a sly negative thought crept in without you realising, when you least expected it. All your life, negative thinking has been your default mechanism. This could be due to your childhood experiences, self-esteem that was never fully realised, putting others before you or just being in toxic company for long periods of time. There could be a multitude of reasons for this, and there are corresponding triggers as well.

Now you feel yourself slipping into the rabbit hole of negativity. There doesn't seem to be a way out. Strangely, you're tempted to go deeper because you're in familiar territory. Your negative thoughts are multiplying and feeding off one another. They're provoking negative emotions. Soon, you're overwhelmed with anger, regret, grief, guilt, jealousy, hurt or a combination of feelings that are energetically low in vibration.

You can't seem to get a grip of yourself because you've lost control. You're completely lost in the ocean of toxicity. You can't understand why it's happening because you've worked so hard to avoid feeling this way. It is a vicious cycle. You thought you'd put an end to it, but here it is again!

You feel emotionally drained and physically exhausted. Your mind is conjuring undesirable images that make you feel worse. Your mind is working overtime and exploring its creative potential. You don't know what to do. You're not able to do anything productive. You've nothing nice to say. You've nothing nice to think. You don't feel like talking to anyone because you know that you could end up feeling worse. You're stuck in a lose-lose situation.

This is certainly not a desirable state to be in. You've got to understand something. There will always be the possibility of negative thoughts occurring. It's your job to be alert enough to identify the triggers. Don't fall prey to the temptation that you've been there done that, so you'll be immune to their impact. Never underestimate your triggers and what they can lead you to do. How you handle them is a lifelong process. It's definitely not a one-off action. You've got to keep working on neutralising your triggers every time they come up.

The negative voice in your head will always be working hard to make you feel bad. It's up to you to make the choice to ignore it. That's really tough! I admit. But it's far from impossible. Your mind can be your greatest ally or your strongest enemy. You get to choose what it'll be because you are not your mind. You control it. When you're dragged down by emotions and challenges, you become more vulnerable to negative thinking. I don't believe that it's possible to completely eradicate negative thoughts. However, it's my conviction that you can prevent them from getting the better of you.

As long as you exist, negative thoughts will keep sprouting in your mind, especially when you least expect it. The trick is to catch them red-handed. What do I mean by this? The moment you recognise and identify a thought to be negative, call it out. Question it. Challenge it. Be acutely aware that it's not what you actually think. Be aware that it's your mind orchestrating unfavourable scenarios, provoking you to act in unfavourable ways – provoking you to sabotage yourself.

Tell your mind, 'I know exactly what you're up to! You may have managed to control me so far. But I'm not letting you win again. No way are you going to mess with me!' Know that you're not your mind. You're the one who controls it.

Don't try to resist negative thoughts. The more you resist, the stronger they become. Let them pass through, and be wary of them renting mental space. Allow them to be fleeting thoughts. Never entertain them. Make sure that these toxic thoughts remain out of your energy field. You'll get better at this the more you do it and with time. Sooner rather than later, you will have mastered the skill of handling negative thoughts. You will have more control over what you sieve from your mind. Persevere. Practise until you achieve mastery!

Be prepared for negativity to creep in when you least expect it, even when you're feeling extremely happy and positive. Why? Because you won't be caught off guard. You'll be far less likely to react based on those negative thoughts. You'll be ready to silence them because now you know what to expect. You'll not hurt yourself by entertaining them.

After all, it's your mind working hard to manipulate you. Once you make it clear that you're the master of your mind and not the slave, it simply cannot go against your will.

Take charge of your mind. Take charge of your thoughts. Take charge of your life. Don't fall prey to illusions!

Negativity eats you up from within. It destroys your confidence and self-esteem. It compromises self-worth. You'll begin rejecting aspects of yourself. You may even feel ashamed. You'll feel that you can never match up. You'll never feel enough. Therefore, you'll have major problems accepting yourself. This is just the tip of the iceberg. Negativity has the potential to do so much more harm if you allow it.

I want you to cut yourself some slack. You're human. There will be ups and downs in life. You will feel low vibrational emotions. You will think low vibrational thoughts. All I'm asking of you is not to allow them to linger or even reside within you for good. Get it out of your system as fast as you can. You need to know what it is, how it feels and what it can do. You need the experience. Why? Because it'll make you that much better at handling it the next time it pays a visit.

Be aware of every thought passing through your mind. Be wary of anything that causes emotional discomfort or heaviness. You don't need that burden. Put it down and move forward.

SELF-CRITICISM AND SELF-JUDGEMENT ARE MANIFESTATIONS OF SELF-REJECTION. ACCEPT YOURSELF WITHOUT CONDITIONS OR COMPARISONS. ONLY THEN WILL SELF-EMPOWERMENT BECOME YOUR REALITY. — MEERA JHOGASUNDRAM

PHOTO BY: MEERA JHOGASUNDRAM

Chapter Four

LOVING YOURSELF IS EASY

Congratulations! You're still with me. I know you're determined to get this right. I know how deeply you want to make changes to yourself and in your life for the best. You are committed. That isn't all. You're aligned with your true desires and goals in the best way that you possibly can be presently. How do I know this? If you've read the first three chapters, at the very least you will have experienced an awareness that has been out of your focus till now. You will have experienced a shift in perspective – doesn't matter how big or small it is. You will have been prompted to confront your limitations and accept more of yourself. You will be motivated to rely more on your intuition, and thus yourself. You will know why you should respect yourself first. Above all, you will think about gratitude more, even if you don't get to practise it as often as you'd like to. These are the beginnings of a huge transformation. Bit by bit, one step at a time, you're getting there. Where? Where you will be able to live your best life in your own unique journey, in your own unique way.

By the way, you're just beginning. Trust the process and enjoy it. Don't be in a hurry to get to the end. The beauty lies more in the experience you gain than the destination you reach. You've got some basic tools to understand your worth and value. The next step would be to love yourself unconditionally. I know what you're thinking. Why does it always have to be 'unconditional'? Because my dear friend, if there are going to be conditions, you might as well not get down to doing it. If you have to fulfil a condition before you can love yourself, that is no longer self-love. It's a bargain! It's a sign of self-rejection. It means you think and feel that you're not enough. So, no strings attached. No clauses. No compromises. Love yourself deeply for who you are – just the way you are. This is easier if you've been following my suggestions in the first three chapters.

Often, we're so engrossed in loving something or someone that we conveniently forget to nourish ourselves emotionally. We're eager to do more than expected at work or in personal relationships for the sake of appreciation and approval. There's nothing wrong with this. It's human nature. It backfires when we don't give ourselves the same appreciation and approval. What does loving yourself actually mean? How do you know if you're loving yourself? Is there a tangible way to measure this? I'd say that self-love is a beautiful emotion that you experience when you're taking care of yourself in the best way possible – mentally, emotionally and spiritually. Your needs have to be fulfilled first before you fulfil the needs of your loved ones. You can't pour from an empty cup. You have to be fine and well so that you can do your best for those who matter to you, in order for them to be fine and well. If you try to compromise your welfare so that you can give more of yourself to others, sooner rather than later, you're bound to experience a burnout. You will end up feeling frustrated. You may even feel that you're being taken for granted. That will hurt your relationships.

You teach people how to treat you by the way you treat yourself. The same principle applies for self-love, self-respect, and self-acceptance. When you're giving yourself the love, care and attention that you deserve, you'll never feel drained – mentally, emotionally or spiritually – when you encounter challenges. This has nothing to do with being selfish. It has everything to do with looking after yourself to the best of your ability so that you can give your best to those around you and society. Don't you want to give your best? Don't you want to be your best self, if not always, as often as you can? Self-love is a choice you make to honour yourself because you deserve it. You are worthy. You matter. Before I tell you the 'how to,' I'd like to share a bit of my experience in the self-love journey. Yes, it's a journey. You've got to keep doing it. You've got to keep loving yourself no matter what happens. If you've been given a chance to experience life on this planet, you deserve to be loved by yourself first.

You may think that you love yourself. You may even say it to yourself. How can you be sure that you are genuinely loving yourself? How can you love yourself? What can you do for yourself so that you feel loved? There's really no benchmark. Each person is unique. Ask yourself,

- What makes me smile spontaneously?
- What excites me?
- What relaxes me?
- What makes me feel special?
- What makes me feel confident?
- What makes me feel that I matter?
- What makes me feel that I can make a difference?
- What gives me joy?
- What fulfils me?
- What makes me feel that I'm enough?

These are some questions to help you figure out how you can love yourself best, your way. While you do this, I have specific suggestions that you may wish to consider just to get you started. Now is the best time to start loving yourself.

Self-care is the best route to self-love. You can never go wrong with this. Often, we don't even realise that we're depriving ourselves of the care we deeply desire. We're so engrossed in what has to be done that we overlook what needs to be done first. I'm sure you have your own definition of self-care. Whatever that may be, my questions for you are: Are you taking good care of yourself? Are your self-care methods based on what others think you deserve and should do, or are they truly how you'd like to care for yourself? You are the only person who has the right to decide what you deserve. It's really up to you.

It's so important to love yourself when you don't succeed (when you fall short of your own expectations). When I was in my mid-thirties, I signed up for horse-riding lessons. This had been a dream since childhood. It never materialised when I was younger because the elite clubs offering lessons were beyond my budget and I couldn't find suitable alternatives. Besides, when I was a minor, my mother would never have allowed me to pursue this sport simply because she had always known it to be an extremely dangerous sport. In my thirties, she couldn't stop me, but I know that she silently feared the consequences of a possible permanent injury. When it came to me, her intuition was always spot on. I'll let you in on this just a little more.

Let's travel back to the point in time when I was nine years old and obsessed with playing a game called 'Zero-Point'. It's basically a long string of rubber bands that would be stretched and held horizontally by two of my friends at different levels of height – knee level, waist level, shoulder level, ear level, head level, and even higher than that. My other friends and I would compete, jumping over the horizontal line of stretched rubber bands. At that age, it was so thrilling and exciting to jump over the line every time it was held higher. I was great at it. I had the advantage of being taller than most of my friends. It made me feel good about myself. At home, if I wasn't doing my homework, I would be playing Zero-Point, tying the ends of the string to two different objects (whatever I could find). I would then increase the height after every successful jump-over. I had a few falls, nothing serious. From the moment I took to this game, my mother cautioned me. She told me not to play Zero-Point because I could fall on my face and break my teeth.

Do you think I listened to her? Do you think I took what she said seriously? Absolutely not! I was so good at it and just not prepared to sacrifice the joy I derived from playing it. I continued playing, especially during break time at school. The better I got, the higher the target. One fateful morning while playing Zero-Point at school, I felt ambitious. I told my two tall friends to hold the line of rubber bands as high as possible. I went for it and ended up face down on a tarmac surface (broken stone mixed with tar). The impact and pain were so great that I took a few minutes to understand what had happened. My face was covered with blood. I could feel my teeth moving in my mouth.

I had broken my jaw and my teeth. I couldn't move for some time. I can't remember how I was taken to the sick bay at school. I remember my father coming to the sick bay and carrying me to his car to see the doctor. Prior to that, I had never seen my father look so grave, tense and worried. I remember his eyes being red. He fetched my mother from the school at which she was teaching. When she saw me, she couldn't stop crying. Years later, I realised that it must have been a horrifying sight to behold. At that point, I felt pain and knew that I was injured, but I didn't know the seriousness of my injury.

Cutting a long story short, I had to live with a plastic cast supporting my upper and lower jaw for a year. Meaning, I could only consume liquid food. I couldn't chew. That was bad! It was a very painful experience. I found the frequent visits to the dentist especially torturous, given the numerous injections on my gums that I had to endure. I remember screaming in pain. Bottom line – my mother was absolutely right. I fell on my face and broke my teeth! The point I'd like to make is a mother's intuition is always spot on!

At the age of nine, I don't think I had any idea of the concept of self-love. Now, upon looking back, I can tell you that I didn't love myself enough. How do I know this? Because I didn't value myself, my safety. I chose to disregard warnings and go down the danger zone. Yes, I was a child and children make mistakes. At the same time, there were other children my age who never took the same risks. They valued their safety more, perhaps without even knowing that they were doing so. They knew when to stop. They knew when not to cross the line. They loved themselves enough to save themselves from suffering the pain and trauma of a broken jaw. You may think that I'm being too hard on myself. Let me make it clear. Self-love starts at a very young age. As you grow older, you'll realise that you can't have lasting success in any area of your life without loving yourself first. Self-love is not selfish. It is a basic, fundamental element of self-care.

My mother's intuition told her something similar when I told her that I was signing up for horse-riding lessons. She tried to caution me, but I wasn't prepared to give up my childhood dream. In the three years that I spent learning horse riding, I had five falls. The second fall was the most dangerous. While learning to canter, I lost balance and clung to the horse's neck. The horse continued to canter, and I slid to the ground. Up to that point, all was fine. When I was on the ground, the horse's hoof hit my head gear and cracked it. For about thirty minutes, I didn't know what I was doing. To date, I have no recollection of what I did during those minutes. I suffered a concussion. I didn't know at that point that it was a concussion. I got back on the horse because that's what we were taught to do to overcome our fears. I cantered a few rounds. I still can't believe that I did that without making mistakes, because in actual fact, I didn't know what was going on. I can't remember cantering after the fall. It's just erased from my memory.

On my way home, I felt movement inside my head. It wasn't painful. It was very uncomfortable. I was advised to go for a medical examination. I was hospitalised for a one-day observation. The doctor ordered a scan, and I was warned never to fall again. I still remember thinking to myself, 'Who would actually choose to fall?' I didn't go for horse-riding lessons for about two weeks. After that, I became even more determined to get back on the horse. I wasn't going to quit. I wasn't going to give up on my childhood dream. I wasn't prepared to accept the fact that horse riding was becoming too risky. I went back for lessons.

It took me a good three years and five falls before I eventually stopped horse-riding lessons. I can't explain why or how, but somehow, I managed to attach my self-worth to the fulfilment of my childhood dream. I wasn't going to feel good enough if I didn't make it as an equestrian at some level. I just wasn't prepared to accept myself if I stopped training. There was so much resistance to facing the stark truth. The fact of the matter was that fear was gradually building within me after each fall. By the time I got to the third fall, I had enough fear to cause a conflict of emotions within me. On one hand, I wanted to go as far as possible in this sport. On the other hand, I knew that I was losing confidence and gaining fear.

You must be wondering what my horse-riding experience has to do with loving myself. Valid thought. I learned that one of the most important and effective ways of loving myself is to know what to quit and when to quit. This has nothing to do with never giving up. Let me explain. When you've decided to pursue a certain course of action after careful consideration, when you have a good idea of the direction in which you're heading, when you know that you are serious about your pursuit, and when your determination and drive increases with time, by all means, go for it! If your interest or passion evolves into a source of fear, stress or lack of worth, and it compromises your well-being, that's when you've got to seriously reconsider your decision. In my case, I eventually grew to love myself enough to quit something that was evoking increasing fear. Perhaps I had too many falls to remain confident. Perhaps I feared the risk of suffering a permanent disability due to a fall. Perhaps I could have pursued the sport for a longer period if I had started training when I was much younger. There could be many reasons. But you know what? Whatever the reason, it really doesn't matter.

What matters is the fact that I don't need to achieve something or do more of something to love myself. I am enough as I am. I am worthy of feeling great about myself because I am unique. There is only one me. That goes for you too. Don't attach your worth to anything other than the person you are in your element. If an action compromises your well-being, choose yourself over it. Love yourself enough to quit. Be proud of yourself that you gave it a fair shot. Be proud of yourself that you did your best; you persevered as much as you could. Be grateful for the experience and move forward doing what's best for you, always aspiring to become the best version of yourself.

I understand that there's a lot of stereotyping and taboo associated with quitting. Quitters are likened to losers. If you quit, you're branded as a failure. This is society's superficiality at its best. Don't fall for it. I quit my job after more than 20 years fighting the odds. Would you consider me to be a failure? What you think of yourself matters most. What you think of yourself comes first. Anything that makes you feel and think less of yourself is not worth your attention. Value yourself. Love yourself. Understand and know that quitting can be one of the best acts of self-love, depending on your situation.

Apart from knowing what to quit and when to quit, I have a few suggestions on how you can love yourself, guaranteed to help you. I know that loving yourself isn't as easy as it sounds. You have to check yourself and be intentional when you practise these suggested acts of self-love.

1. BE KIND TO YOURSELF

You're falling behind on the list of things you need to do every day. You keep postponing the uncompleted tasks to the following day, and you're struggling to keep up. To top it off, you're extremely exhausted. You don't know why you always end up in this position. I'm not talking about procrastination. I'm referring to a genuine case of unrealistic expectations for yourself.

When coming up with a daily schedule, we often overestimate our capacity and underestimate distractions or unexpected occurrences that are part of life. We disregard our emotional well-being and mental state on any particular day. What do I mean by this? Let me explain.

You may be feeling worn out when you wake up in the morning because you didn't get enough sleep. You may have woken up several times during the night. You're having a headache. You can't concentrate. You can't get as much work done as you had planned to. It would be unkind of you to chide yourself for falling short of expectations. Look at the situation. Understand your needs. Understand how and when you function best. Give yourself a little leeway.

Take a break. Give yourself a small treat. It could be your favourite meal or dessert. Whatever perks you up. It's likely that your schedule doesn't include a breather. That could be building pressure and preventing you from working at a pace that's most productive for you. It's OK not to meet the mark once in a while. It's OK to make mistakes. It's OK to treat yourself even when you think you don't deserve it. It's OK to be kind to yourself. It's OK to love yourself for your imperfections.

There are so many ways in which you can be kind to yourself, every day, in everything you do. And kindness is only one aspect of self-care. Don't mistake self-care for complacency. You're a thinking, feeling human, not a machine. Even machines break down. Being hard on yourself isn't going to make you feel loved. It's not going to bring out the best in you.

When you are kind to yourself, you will be kind to those around you. If someone isn't kind to you, just make sure that you continue being kind to yourself. You decide how you should be treated, not anyone else.

2. *REWARD YOURSELF*

I can't stress this enough. It's so important to celebrate the small wins in life. I'm talking about your small wins every day. Perhaps you've completed the introduction to your presentation and you're feeling great. You're feeling a deep sense of accomplishment. Don't qualify your feelings by telling yourself that it's just an introduction and that you're not even halfway through the presentation. Make sure you celebrate this small win. Watch something you like, eat something you've been craving, or dance to your favourite song. I don't know what celebration means to you. It really doesn't matter how you celebrate. Just do it!

3. *DON'T JUDGE YOURSELF*

You didn't get the promotion you've been working so hard for. You made sure all the boxes were ticked. You've been looking forward to a boost in your career for a long time. The one who was promoted is far less qualified than you, both academically and professionally. You're left feeling inadequate, insulted and disappointed. You begin re-examining yourself, your work performance and your achievements. You make comparisons that only aggravate your frustration. You begin criticising yourself for aiming for that promotion. You begin judging yourself for not moving up the corporate ladder after so long.

This is exactly what you shouldn't be doing if you love yourself. There are numerous reasons for someone being promoted over you. Your worth is not determined by a single promotion. You are worth much more. Your life is worth much more. This is the perfect opportunity to take a step back and decide on the direction in which you want to move forward. Stop blaming yourself. Stop judging yourself. Quit being harsh with yourself. You certainly don't deserve it.

Perhaps it's best that you choose a new direction. One that leads you to fulfilment. Perhaps this is the Universe giving you a wake-up call. Perhaps it's time for a reality check and time for you to move out of your comfort zone. You've got to believe that the Universe is your best ally. If something you're trying so hard for is refusing to manifest itself, trust that it's nature's way of telling you that you're meant for something else far better. I'm choosing to refer to the cosmic energy as the Universe. Whatever you identify with as the power that is infinitely greater than you, that's what I'm referring to as the Universe. Feel free to adapt this concept to suit your existing beliefs. I'll go into the details of trusting the Universe in Chapter Five. I just had to mention it for this example.

How can changing your perspective of a seemingly unfortunate situation be considered as loving yourself? This brings me to my next point…

4. MOTIVATE YOURSELF WHENEVER YOU FEEL UNMOTIVATED

You're human. It's natural to feel low-vibrational emotions such as grief, anger, disappointment, jealousy, anxiety, worry, etc. What's important is that you make a conscious effort to come out of that emotional state as soon as you possibly can. This can be tricky. You've got to give yourself the time and space to heal from a particular low-vibrational feeling. If you rush this process, you would be depriving that emotional wound from healing. You would be sabotaging yourself. How? In the future, when you least expect it, old wounds will cut you deeper and stronger at the slightest trigger. You're likely to go back to ground zero. Only this time, you may take a longer time to heal, even if you allow yourself to completely heal.

Why is healing so important? Because if you let something like low self-esteem linger too long in your system, your energy field, you will lose motivation. You will feel drained even when you've not done anything productive the entire day. You will feel that you're not good enough. You won't see a point in carrying on with whatever you're doing. You're very likely to be complacent, even lazy. Nothing will seem to be working out in your favour. You won't expect to succeed, and therefore, the amount of effort you make will be compromised. You will stop yourself from realising and achieving your full potential. Isn't this sabotaging yourself?

When motivation is lost, your behaviour falls into the trap of a vicious cycle. You've lost your spark, so you don't accomplish what you're supposed to, or you procrastinate. Because you're not able to see the end product of your goal, you lack the drive to go on. You lose both ways. If you're entangled in this web of delusion, you better free yourself as soon as you can. You owe it to yourself.

It's not real. It's your mind manipulating you, making sure that you remain stuck. Refuse to be stuck. Refuse to be unmotivated. I know what you're thinking. Sounds great, but how exactly do you do this effectively? I have a few suggestions. I trust that you'll find them helpful.

Divert attention.

The moment you begin thinking less of yourself, divert your attention to something that you're really good at. Instead of focusing on everything that's not working in your life, shift your focus to what has worked great for you in the past and do that. It could be something totally unrelated to what you're supposed to work on presently. For instance, you could be working on a sales pitch and you can't seem to pen down the details because you've lost confidence. You've not closed a sale in months. You've begun doubting yourself. You're no longer motivated. Please don't pause and linger on that feeling of inadequacy. Immediately do something that makes you laugh, excites you, and energises you. Do something that makes you feel good about yourself. Perhaps you love to dance and you haven't had the chance to do that in a while.

Don't think twice. Do your favourite moves to your favourite music. They don't have to be perfect. No one's watching. It's just you reminding yourself of how great you are, getting in touch with who you truly are. When you're done, you'll feel exhausted, but you'll also experience something amazing – the feeling of joy and accomplishment. You've shifted your mind from what's not working to what's working so well and so easily.

When you're in this state of positive emotion, don't let go of that feeling. Build on it. Get out of the house. Pay a visit to your street food stall. Get that spicy sandwich that always perks you up. Spend a few hours outside doing things that are not in any way related to whatever is not working for you presently. Don't get back to the sales pitch until the following day or until you feel much better. You're basically taking a break. I've given you specific examples because how you take a break matters. You're not going to experience much change if you remain in the environment in which that one thing was not working out for you. You've got to move. You've got to change the way you're feeling quickly.

- *REASSESS YOUR DIRECTION.*

Diverting your attention works very well if you're headed in the direction that's best for you. If you find yourself constantly stalling and procrastinating, you've got to pay attention to the underlying message. I wouldn't know the specific message intended for you, but I can suggest that you take a long, hard look at what you're presently doing and where you're heading. Are you doing what you want to do? You don't have to be passionate about it, but at the very least, you've got to like it. Where do you see yourself in the next few years? Doing whatever you're doing right now? Can you see yourself living the life you desire? How is this going to help you achieve your long-term goals?

If you don't have long-term goals, I suggest you start thinking about them. I've some questions to guide you. What brings out the best in you? What gives you a sense of achievement? What allows your imagination and creativity to thrive? What makes you feel that you're making a significant contribution to society, to humanity, or even to our planet? By the way, this doesn't mean that you're not living in the moment. It ensures that every moment is meaningfully lived. Allowing nature to take its course is important. At the same time, it's your duty to do the best you can. You owe it to yourself to discover what truly keeps the spark in you alive. You are the only one responsible for your life. You have the power to co-create your destiny with the Universe as your best ally.

If whatever you're doing now gives you a bleak picture of the future or, even worse, you're unable to see where you're heading in the near future, this is a clear sign that what you're doing right now is not serving your best interest. Ask yourself – why am I doing this? Is there something else I'd rather be doing? Am I going to live a compromised life by editing myself and my potential to fulfil others' expectations? What is my expectation for myself in the next five years? What means the most to me? What am I willing to give up in order to pursue my interests?

If you're unable to see yourself living the life you wish to in the next few years or even in the long run, reassess the way you're getting work done right now. Is there something you can change? Do you have a balanced lifestyle? Are you working all the time without any play or are you taking too much time for leisure? Are you exercising? This is an excellent way to increase motivation. You could even call it a magic formula. How do you feel after a good workout? I know you'd be exhausted. I also know that you'd be feeling rejuvenated. You'd be feeling great about yourself. That's how you should always think and feel about yourself. What can you change about your lifestyle, your routine, that will get you excited about all the things you'd like to accomplish? Remember, all the answers are within you. You've got to trust your intuition, listen attentively to the answers and follow the guidance.

Find creative ways to complete your task. How can you add your personal touch to it? How can you make it unique? Do it your way and claim ownership. It's likely that you're disconnected from your project. Once you make it an extension of who you are, your creativity and talent, you will have a desire to complete it to the best of your ability. That's you motivating yourself!

* ***GET REAL.***

One of the most popular reasons for losing motivation is to have unrealistic expectations. You've got to understand that working smart and taking the shortcut are two different things. There are some steps in life that you just can't afford to skip. And if you do, you'll end up having too many steps back because you haven't learned the ropes of the trade well enough. For instance, if you lack the skills and experience required for a particular job, it's impractical to expect a high salary when you're just getting started. You may not even get the job. Be realistic about what point you're at right now. Accept your shortcomings. Improve on them. Upgrade yourself. Meanwhile, apply for a position that's more suitable for you now, not one that you may qualify for in a few years. Get real!

Social media can either be a boon or a bane. It depends on how you sieve the overwhelming information. Don't be taken in by the countless posts on captivating lifestyles, dream jobs, dream vacations and dream houses. They're basically advertisements and are often sponsored or have an attached paid promotion. Don't be influenced by the impressive jobs and attractive salaries of your relatives, friends and people in your social circle. Don't succumb to peer pressure. Basically, don't compare yourself with anyone.

Your inclinations, capabilities and potential are unique to you. That is why, as I mentioned earlier, it's so important to take another look at what you're doing and where you're heading. If it doesn't allow you to grow and evolve into the best version of yourself, you're probably not making full use of your strengths. You have to be absolutely honest with yourself about what you can do, how much you can do, and when you can do it. If you set goals and targets based on others' achievements, you're setting yourself up for failure.

When you set a deadline for yourself, be sure to take into consideration your attention span and the environment in which you work most productively. If you have to complete a written assignment, plan a schedule based on your tendencies. What do I mean by this? Think about these questions: Are you the kind of person who can write nonstop for two hours? Or do you have to stop and take a break after thirty minutes? Do you like to exercise at the end of the day, after completing your tasks? Or do you prefer exercising first thing in the morning? How often do you do your grocery shopping? How long do you take to prepare and have lunch? How often do you go out for leisure in a week? If you fall ill, do you give yourself time to recover? Do you allocate specific times for social media engagements?

If you work best at night, there's no point in rising at five a.m. and forcing yourself to do things just because someone said you should. You'll be miserable. If you have a short attention span, there's no point in planning a timetable for three hours of continuous writing every day. If you're the kind of person who has to get out of the house at least once a day, you better make time for that because it will keep you going so that you can do your best. Please don't deprive yourself of what's best for you.

On the same note, if you know that you need to upgrade yourself for a particular job, you can either apply for a lower position now or you could wait until you've acquired the necessary qualifications. You're bound to be disappointed if you apply for a position that you're underqualified for. It's the perfect recipe to become unmotivated and think less of yourself when your application is rejected. It's the perfect excuse to give up, and with time, become complacent. It's you sabotaging yourself. This is the second time I'm talking about the 'unrealistic job expectation', and there's a reason for it. I've seen so many people young and middle-aged wallow in self-pity and disappointment because they didn't manage to secure their desired job. Talking to them brought to light their unrealistic expectations based on their qualifications.

With reference to the same point I made earlier, don't judge yourself by where you are now. Believe that you are where you're meant to be. Learn the lessons well. Improve yourself. Focus on yourself minus the distraction of what everybody else is doing. It's up to you whether you move forward, remain stagnant, or slide backwards. You have to make the effort, and you have to be honest about how much work you need to put in. You have to be honest about your limitations. You have to be honest about how far you can go within a given time frame. Please get real with yourself! Otherwise, sooner rather than later, you're going to lose motivation. And you won't be able to figure out why because you've been lying to yourself about the little things that matter – the little things about yourself. When you're true to yourself, even if you lose the spark somewhere down the road, you'll be able to refuel your drive to go forward.

5. *SET HEALTHY BOUNDARIES.*

Having healthy boundaries is a gamechanger, especially if you have strong people-pleasing tendencies. It is also a fool proof way of loving yourself unconditionally. If you do everything that I've suggested so far and somehow manage to still have weak boundaries, all your efforts will be in vain. Learning to say no to things and people that don't serve your highest good is an art all by itself. There are some who're able to say no, but they end up feeling guilty and bad for doing so. There are others who say no, and after spending some time pondering, they substitute it with an unhealthy yes. Whoever benefits from the yes gets their work done. What about the one who says yes? Her time, money, resources, and overall well-being is compromised. You may think that this is an exaggeration. Let me explain.

When you know that you have far more important things to attend to and you stretch yourself to do favours for others, something has got to give. And it's always something to do with your well-being. You could have completed your assignment. You could have gone out for a long walk in your favourite forest. This is time in nature that should not be sacrificed! You could have gone to bed earlier and had a long overdue, much-needed rest. You could have cooked your favourite meal and enjoyed dinner. You could have continued reading the novel that you badly want to get back to. These may seem trivial compared to the favour you agreed to do. Remember, they're trivial for the person you're helping. They are your necessities!

Like I mentioned earlier in this book, you've got to respect yourself first. This means that your needs and wants must be attended to first. You've got to be fine and well before you can make a positive difference in the lives of those around you (those near and dear to you). If you prioritise others' needs over yours, who's going to look out for you? Your intuition would have done its job, I'm sure. But did you listen to it? Did you follow its guidance? You know at your gut level that you're not up for obliging others anymore. You know this because it drains you of your energy. You're deprived of doing the things that will make your life easier and better. Why would you want to do that?

How do you set healthy boundaries?

6. DON'T CHANGE TO FIT IN.

You find it appealing to be part of a certain group. You think it elevates your social status. You want to feel included and accepted. You want to feel liked and popular. You think you'll have a stronger voice because of strong support. Ultimately, you want to feel good about yourself. You want to feel a sense of belonging. You want that connection.

At the same time, you know that the behaviour of people in this group are not aligned with your values and principles. For instance, they could be unjustly critical of others and even display condescension. You can see that they are always pointing fingers at others when things go wrong. You find that they are superficial in their friendships. Yet, they get the attention they want. People listen to what they have to say. They're confident. Their wealth and social status fuel their influence. They are recognised by others for obvious reasons. They make it clear to others that it's a privilege to be part of their inner circle.

You know that you would have to edit your behaviour, hide your likes and dislikes, compromise your authenticity, and even change your personality to fit into the group. Would you go ahead and do it? Let's break this apart. You may have a stronger voice, but do you think that will be your authentic voice? Will it be what you stand for? Will it represent you accurately? Before you connect with others, do you check if you're firmly connected with yourself? Meaning, are you grounded in your values and principles (whatever is most important to you)? Do you respect yourself enough to be comfortable in your own skin? Do you believe in yourself enough to stand up for what you believe in?

In your mind, without anyone's influence, are you clear about what kind of person you want to be? Is that aligned with the kind of person you're portraying yourself to be? Do you respect people and your relationships or are they just a means to an end? Do you love yourself enough to be unapologetically true to yourself?

These are hard questions you've got to answer before attempting to change yourself in order to fit into a group. I can't say this enough. Own your uniqueness. Your soul tribe will align themselves with you in time to come. When you attempt to alter your personality, not only are you compromising your character, you're also sabotaging your well-being.

Trying to be someone you're not will suffocate your individuality in no time. You'll end up feeling like you're living a lie. You will lose meaning in life because you've strayed from what makes you special. You will be dissatisfied, frustrated, and even angry at yourself for putting yourself on the back burner.

• *HAVE GOALS UNIQUE TO YOU.*

When you are part of a community, activity or team, the interaction is bound to have some impact on you. No one has to demand that you think a certain way. No one has to force you to do things a certain way.

The exchange of ideas, opinions and expectations somehow enter your system. Who knows, it could even be registered in your subconscious mind. This may influence your goals, both long-term and short-term.

The purpose of having goals is to push you the extra mile so that you can explore your potential. If your goals are crafted based on others' achievements, aspirations and interests, you risk settling for less than what you can aim for – what you ought to aim for. It could be worse. Meaning, you pursue something that is not attracting your complete involvement. There is nothing wrong with mediocrity if it's a choice. If you're compelled to settle for mediocrity because your heart and soul is not in whatever you're pursuing, you're going to end up feeling frustrated. You risk thinking less of yourself. Once you start doing this, you will fall into the vicious cycle of self-criticism, self-judgement and demotivation. You risk compromising your self-worth and self-esteem. You risk rejecting yourself, making it almost impossible to love yourself.

Why go down that road? Why not make a conscious effort to set goals based on your inclinations, capabilities and desires? So what if they deviate from external expectations? Isn't what you expect from yourself most important? How can you create the life you wish to live based on other people's desires? Be sure to check yourself on this. Be sure to reassess your goals at every milestone. Know exactly why you're pursuing them. If the reason is you and only you, you're on the right track. Don't mistake this for selfishness. This is basic self-care. As I keep saying, you've got to be fine, well and happy before you can make any positive difference in the lives of those who matter to you.

Your goals are an extension of you. They represent your vision for the future. They help define your purpose in life. You recreate yourself through your goals. It's your job to discover what's truly important to you and how you'd like to tap into your potential. You know yourself best. Your goals help you connect with yourself on a deeper level. You connect to the source energy that created you through your goals. Compromising this is not an option.

- ### *BE THE DECISION-MAKER.*

At any point in time, in any situation, be the one to decide what's best for you. Don't give up this right. Sacrificing your freedom to choose so that you can please someone is unacceptable. Sacrificing the right to

YOU ARE THE KEY

stand up for yourself in order to avoid conflict will cage you mentally and spiritually. There is no peace, no fulfilment. This doesn't mean that you shouldn't compromise. Healthy relationships require compromise, which is the opposite of sacrificing your authenticity. In a balanced, give-and-take relationship, you have the right and freedom to decide if you wish to compromise on a certain issue. On the contrary, in a toxic relationship, you would be made to feel guilty for not sacrificing your needs.

Bottom line – you know yourself best. You know your situation best. You owe it to yourself to look out for your best interests. Be mindful that this is not a privilege. It's your basic right. You have to decide what you're willing to settle for and what your non-negotiables are. You have to be comfortable and confident about your decision. At the end of the day, you need your space to live freely. Anyone encroaching on your privacy and freedom is bound to leave you in a state of deep dissatisfaction.

It's difficult for me to spell out exactly what you should be doing in every situation. It all depends on the gravity of the circumstances, the history you have with the people involved, and how much you're willing to compromise. Remember, bending backwards too much may cause a permanent injury. Trust your intuition, respect yourself first, and most importantly, speak your truth; live your truth. You must have the courage to stand up for yourself at all times!

There are little everyday acts of self-love that you may wish to do for yourself. Make at least one meal a day a ritual of loving yourself. Set the table for dinner and light a candle. Enjoy your meal with your favourite dining set. I'm talking about the plate and the fork and spoon that you've been reserving for special occasions. Take it out from the display cabinet and use it for yourself. Make your spicy chai with organic honey to sip and savour, making your dinner even more special. Why not?! After all, you are special. When you go for a walk by the lake, treat yourself to that heavenly pistachio ice cream, in a cone of course. Never mind that it's exorbitantly priced just because it's sold by a vendor in a popular area. Never mind that you could buy more of that same ice cream for a small fraction of the price at your local supermarket. You are soaking in the beauty of nature and you're feeling lovely. Cherish the moment. Honour it by sealing it with something as small and insignificant as a cone of ice cream. Why? Because you deserve it. You are special. You love yourself. When you look back, that simple act of self-love will be one of your most treasured memories, one of your most beautiful moments in nature.

Taking care of your physical self is an amazing way of loving yourself. You don't need to go to the hair salon, but you feel like being pampered. You want to feel relaxed and have someone take care of your crowning glory. You're secretly craving the head massage that goes with the hair wash. Go ahead and pamper yourself! You deserve it because you are worthy. You are special.

These are a few simple ways of making sure that you practise self-love regularly. Find your primary and secondary acts of self-love. Find out what makes you feel loved and give it to yourself as often as you can. Be in a state of receiving, be it love, abundance, opportunities, money, wealth, prosperity, etc. Before you attract these into your life, you've got to believe that you are worthy of them and love yourself unconditionally. Be prudent but don't be stingy with yourself. No matter what happens on the outside, never stop loving yourself on the inside.

CHOOSING WHAT TO QUIT AND WHEN TO QUIT IS SOMETIMES ONE OF THE BEST WAYS OF LOVING YOURSELF. — MEERA JHOGASUNDRAM

Chapter Five

TRUST THE UNIVERSE

L iving in a capitalistic, materialistic world, we're trained very young to expect something in return for whatever we do. Of course, if you're working for an organisation, you would naturally expect to be paid every month for your time and services. Money is actually energy. Being paid for working is actually an exchange of energy. You're taught to expect more energy in return for giving more of your energy. This gives you the illusion that you are in control of the outcome of a situation, be it work or any other situation in your life. Why do I call it an illusion? Because the only thing you're ever going to be able to control is whatever is happening within you.

You can control your beliefs, thoughts and actions. You can control your emotions by choosing your beliefs and thoughts. You can control how you respond to a person or in a particular situation. However, you have no control over anything outside of you. You can't control someone's actions. You can't control how someone thinks and feels about you. You can do your best at work, but whether or not you get promoted is beyond your control. You can do your best to salvage a relationship, but the outcome is beyond your control. You can apply for the best university in the state but actually securing a place is beyond your control. What am I getting at here? You've got to understand and accept that there's only so much you can do.

You are the co-creator of your life; you don't control it. You are the co-creator of your destiny; you don't control it. I believe you've got my message. The beauty of life is in letting go and letting it flow. The beauty of living in the moment is letting it be and cherishing every bit of it. Letting go is such a deep concept that I could go on for hours talking about it. For the purpose of this chapter, I'm condensing the essence of the art of letting go into a few paragraphs. Remember, you can never finish letting go. Just when you think you've let go, something crops up showing you that you're still very attached to the outcome of your desires.

My personal experience with letting go has been a very long and arduous journey. Throughout life, things will happen to you, and you will have to constantly practise the art of letting go. Why is it so important to let go? If you cling to the outcome of a goal or a desire, you'll be stalling yourself from moving forward. You'll be stuck in the rut of expectations, hoping, wanting, and dreaming. Don't get me wrong. Hopes and dreams add beauty to life. It's the 'wanting' that dampens your spirit. Because if you are focused on wanting something, you're actually focusing on what you lack. You're feeding the self-limiting belief that you're not enough. Focusing on lack never brings about abundance. You'll just go deeper and deeper down the well of lack.

So how do you let go of attachment to the outcome of your desires? You've got to trust your intuition. When you trust your inner guidance, you're trusting yourself. When you trust yourself, you're trusting the path in which you're guided to travel. When you trust your path, you're trusting the journey along that path. When you trust your journey, you're trusting the process that takes you from where you are to where you wish to be. When you truly trust the process, you're actually telling the Universe, 'I trust you!' That's right. That's how you let go. That's how you trust the Universe. The Universe refers to the Creator, source energy, lifeforce energy, divine power, etc. However you choose to interpret these, whatever symbols you attach to them, even if you're an atheist, you must know that there is a power greater than you that created you. There is a power that is responsible for creation. This force resonates with different people in different ways.

I happen to have a very good memory. I remember the good stuff and I especially remember bad experiences. In the larger scheme of things, there is no such thing as good and bad. Life is not defined by this duality. Every experience has shaped my life and moulded my character for the best. I am forever grateful for the invaluable lessons I've learned.

Still, to get my point across, I'm making use of the good-bad analogy.

When I received an offer of acceptance for the doctorate programme on international relations, I pretty much decided what my life purpose should be. In my mind, it had to be something to do with migration studies and policy analysis. Why? Because my research proposal at the application stage was on migration – Europe's migration crisis (which isn't actually a crisis as migration is an age-old phenomenon). This issue (sensationalised by international media) piqued my interest at that point in time. After more than two decades of working, I resigned and moved to Geneva, Switzerland, to do my studies full time.

Though I was terrified of taking such a huge leap of faith, I didn't give it a second thought because I desperately wanted a change in life. I badly wanted to do something different. I wanted to explore my academic potential. I wanted to see for myself how I would fare in a PhD course. While preparing to move to Geneva, I was going over all the possible career options in my mind. I came to the conclusion that it would be best to work in an international organisation that specialised in migration policy analysis and research. My second option was to work in a university and eventually become a professor. I had it all figured out and that was it. I wasn't considering anything else. I was not going to keep my options open because as far as I was concerned, I had already discovered what was best for me. I was in complete control of my destiny. So I thought!

It still fascinates me that I never gave enough consideration to my level of interest in migration studies. I decided that I would be specialising in this academic field and that's all that mattered. It's amazing how the Universe orchestrated a series of mostly unpleasant and complicated experiences in order to steer me back to my true path. At this point, I'd like to highlight that migration is a dynamic area to study and work in. However, during my three-year PhD programme, I discovered that I am extremely passionate about climate change issues, environmentalism, wildlife conservation, ocean conservation, nature and photography. These are things I never gave any attention to because I was busy upgrading myself academically and professionally to compete in the corporate rat race. Sad but true!

The more I became engaged in these issues, the more I discovered myself. I believe you know where I've been led. If you're reading my book, you know! While creating awareness of my passion topics on social media platforms such as Twitter, LinkedIn, Facebook, Pinterest, Instagram and my website, I was awakened to an innate desire that I never knew existed prior to that point in my life. I realised and understood that I love putting out my thoughts and lessons learned from personal experiences. I love helping people by motivating them to live their best lives. I love helping them to empower themselves so that they can always aspire to be their best self.

I know what you must be thinking. I agree with you. What I love to do is a completely different world compared to migration studies. I am undoubtedly passionate about environmentalism. Still, I wanted to choose one area to specialise in. I chose motivation and self-empowerment. Why? It's closest to my heart. It's my truth. I have years and years of lived experience motivating, empowering, and picking myself up whenever I fall. I am living my truth by being absolutely honest with myself. It wasn't an easy decision. It took about three years for me to admit it and act on it while writing my doctoral thesis. It's an irony, and a beautiful one too. It taught me crucial life lessons.

I am the co-creator of my destiny, provided I am always true to myself and provided I don't attempt to control the outcome of my actions. I had to learn to let go and let it flow. I had to learn to be honest with myself for every decision I make, in every aspect of my life. I had to learn to have the courage to live my truth. I had to learn to prioritise my true desires over what was expected of me. I had to learn the importance of discovering my true passion. I had to learn that I actually love writing; I learned that I actually love writing a book. It's second nature to me. I had to learn that I love sharing my experiences so that you, on the receiving end, can make better decisions for yourself.

I was overwhelmed. I was scared of failing. It was unfamiliar territory for me. Self-employment was never an option in the past. I believed that I was not cut out for it. Look how life turned out for me! While I am most active on Twitter, I am also present on other social media platforms (YouTube, Instagram, Facebook, my website, Pinterest, LinkedIn) spreading awareness on environmental justice and wildlife conservation, as well as emphasising the importance of motivation and self-empowerment in our daily lives. Currently, my YouTube channel is focused on videos highlighting themes and concepts from this book and upcoming releases in my self-empowerment series. I add value to my followers' experiences with my posts. Through my content, I have

MEERA JHOGASUNDRAM

the opportunity of exploring my creativity frequently. While this may be demanding at times, it is a constant source of nourishment for my soul. While you're reading my first book, I am busy working on the next in my series. Yes, there's more to come, just around the corner. Authoring books will continue for a long time to come, be it on personal development or some other issue that has a strong grasp of my attention. I am finally doing what I am passionate about. I am finally living my truth. I assure you that my journey has been nothing short of beautiful, despite the challenges I've encountered.

So, what does my experience have to do with trusting the Universe? I wish you could see me right now. I'm smiling while writing this. There is a power greater than me that knows what is most suitable for me, what gives me the joy and abundance I desire and deserve (minus all the fluff created by society), what my true path is, what my life purpose is, and what my journey is. That power has inspired me to write this book at this point in my life. I trust that power. I trust the Universe completely.

I can't say that motivation and self-empowerment will be my only areas of focus henceforth and in the distant future. What I can tell you for sure is that I love what I'm doing now. It gives me pure pleasure. It makes me feel so good about myself. I know I'm making a difference in this planet, in my own way. Every word in this book is written with gratitude and enthusiasm. I never lost motivation during the time spent writing it. One of the strongest motivators is the fact that many people are going to benefit from my experiences, in one way or another.

It's when I stopped trying to control who I thought I should become, where I thought I should work, and what I thought I should do for the rest of my life that positive changes began taking place within me, for me, and around me. I had to let go and just exist as my true self (being absolutely honest about what makes me happy). Only then did the power greater than me lead me to my truth, my direction, what's meant for me, and what's best for me. The manner in which this happened was so gradual and complex that I can't even begin to describe my process of awakening. I didn't need to know the how. I just trust this power completely because I know that it's the only way I'll be led to become my best self and live my truth for the rest of my life. If you're lost and you've no clue how to let go, don't worry. I have a few suggestions that can help.

- 70 -

1. *REWARD YOURSELF BEFORE KNOWING THE OUTCOME*

You have a goal that you've been working towards. You have a desired outcome. You've been doing your best to achieve it. You want it so badly, so desperately, that this goal is no longer separate from you. It has become you. Your worth is not attached to it and dependent on it. You're clinging tightly to the expectation of succeeding. You're having sleepless nights over this. You're becoming overly dependent on the specific outcome that you desire.

Your energy is dissipating because you're always thinking about it. You feel exhausted – mentally, emotionally and spiritually. The expectation of the outcome of this goal is overwhelming your life and dominating your thoughts. You're becoming more and more restless and anxious. You're unable to focus on anything else. What do you think you can do? How do you detach from expectations that are increasingly becoming hazardous to your well-being?

I suggest that you reward yourself for the effort you've put in, even before you know the outcome. You deserve to be acknowledged and encouraged. Instead of expecting recognition from others, give it to yourself. You've got to know that you are worthy of your desires. You've got to value yourself by respecting yourself first. Remember, loving yourself is unconditional, regardless of the outcome.

2. *HAVE DIFFERENT INTERESTS*

Perhaps you love photography, but you've been spending all your time on one goal, and you just haven't been able to get back to your passion. This would be an excellent interest to ease your mind. When you're not in the mood to go outdoors, perhaps you could catch up on that favourite novel of yours. You may love feeding animals because it makes you feel more connected to yourself. It fulfils you.

In addition to your daily routine, make it a point to immerse yourself in these activities regularly. Even once a week or a few times a month would make a positive impact on your life. You'll feel great about yourself because you're nourishing your soul. You'll feel fulfilled by several different activities, not just one. You'll have a healthy balance in your life – mentally, emotionally and spiritually. You have to be balanced in all three aspects before you can function optimally. You'll feel that you have spent your time well. Most importantly, your mind will no longer be focused on that one, specific outcome you've worked so hard for.

If your entire life revolves around one specific outcome, you risk needing it. You risk becoming needy. You risk distorting a healthy desire into an obsession. Why let that happen? You've got to understand that you are not your desires, nor are you defined by them. You are so much more than them! Your interests are your saving grace. They help to keep you in an emotionally abundant state. They show you new possibilities.

3. INVEST IN YOURSELF

Imagine what you would like your future to be, at least in the short run. Have a clear picture of the skills you'd like to master. Invest in learning those skills. Invest in yourself. Get busy mastering them. This is personal development. You'll feel good about being responsible. You'll be filled with hope and positive energy. You'll feel motivated.

Your dependence on that one specific goal you've worked so hard for will decrease significantly. Why? Because you're moving forward in life in many different ways. Though you may still have expectations of that specific outcome, you'll become more and more detached from such expectations with every passing day. Your time will be taken up by everything that's working out great for you. Your energy is directed towards investing in yourself. Isn't this your best investment?

Above all, especially after you've done your best, trust the Universe to present to you your desired outcome or something better, in the best possible way. You will not be disappointed. Letting go is an art. It is a lifelong process. The more you practise it, the better you become. For every outcome that you somehow become attached to, practise the art of letting go. After all, you're human. Allow yourself to make mistakes. You will become better with every mistake, every attempt that doesn't succeed. Never give up. At the end of your journey, you'll be grateful and glad that you chose to do your best. You did your best to live your best life. That's what matters most!

Look at it this way. The Universe has led you to my book, to this point in your life where you find yourself doing some soul searching. What you're reading is a catalyst that will speed up positive changes in your life. By now, you should have figured out that I don't believe in coincidences. I've had far too many revelations and miracles happen in my life teaching me the truth that the Universe presents infinite possibilities. I had to do my inner work to make sure that I'm open to these possibilities, though I may have no clue what they actually are. I learned to have faith even though I'm unable to see the whole picture. Honestly, I don't know if I'll reach the spiritual level empowering me to see the entire picture. At the point where I'm at now, it really doesn't matter because I have learned to trust the Universe completely.

When I make such a claim, I want you to understand exactly what I mean. Does it mean that I'll never have low-vibrational thoughts? Certainly not. Does it mean that I'm better than anyone else? Absolutely not. Does it mean that I'm spiritually advanced, or as some may loosely call it, enlightened? Of course not. When I say that I trust the Universe completely, it means that I've learned to let go. By letting go, I'm making life easier, smoother, and even more beautiful for myself. For I know that the Universe will always give me what's best for me when I'm ready to receive it. Knowing that you're worthy isn't enough. You've got to be ready to receive your manifested desires.

Though I've learned to let go of outcomes, it doesn't mean that I will always spontaneously practise it. I continue to learn, and I'm still in the process of mastering it. It can get challenging at times. Life happens, and I do get thrown off balance. I still do get attached to the outcomes of my desires. I still do get attached to my expectations for different aspects of my life. During such times, I make a conscious effort to check myself. I remind myself that the only thing I will ever be able to control is that which goes on within me. I remind myself that I have absolutely no control over anyone else. I keep reminding myself that I have no control over the outcome.

This can be tricky when nothing seems to be working out my way or for me. All the more, I pull myself together and move forward because it's my conviction that the best is yet to come. And as you may already know, our thoughts are extremely powerful. If we train the mind persistently to think positively, we're bound to achieve positive outcomes. Rather, the best outcomes for us. Remember, what's best for you is different from what's best for someone else. So stop comparing!

You have your own path. You have your own growth process. Focus on that. Make the most of the invaluable experiences along the way. Keep thinking about how you can do things better for yourself. Do a regular reality check to make sure that you're in alignment with what's most important to you. Always be willing to learn and evolve. Always be open to change. Always be open to receiving the gifts of the Universe at every milestone, be they tangible or intangible. These should keep you fully occupied and on the right track – the track meant for you. You won't have time for meaningless comparisons.

One of the underlying themes of my book is the need to embrace change. You've been following me on this journey. You have an idea of the numerous changes that I had to accept and work with. If you're not willing to change, it would mean that you're not willing to live. Change is the only constant in life. We're here to learn, grow, evolve and transform into our best self. I understand that it can be challenging to step into unfamiliar territory. I know from the numerous reality checks along my journey that complacency is a trap hidden in the comfort zone. I was stuck for a long time. My wish for you is to avoid such delays. Life is unpredictable, short and far too precious.

It can be life-changing in a positive way to embrace change. You need to know how to do this and be prepared. The sooner, the better. The most drastic changes usually don't come with a warning. Change can hit you any time in the form of unforeseen circumstances. I've learned that whatever happens, it's for the best. There are dreadful incidents and accidents that occur in people's lives. I know that while facing such changes, it would be almost impossible to see how something so terrible could be for the best. Therein lies the strength of faith. Trust the power greater than you. Trust yourself to adapt to changes. To put it bluntly – trusting the Universe completely is one of the best things you could do for yourself, provided you're open and willing to embrace change. Let me suggest three effective ways of doing this.

- *MAKE CHANGE WORK FOR YOU.*

Reframe your thoughts about every change you face. When you're required to change, find ways to benefit from the change. What do you have to do in order to use the change to your advantage? How can you complement the change instead of contradicting it? Do you have to shift to another city or country? Do you have to upgrade your skills? Do you have to start from scratch all over again? Do you have to let go of a lifestyle that no longer serves you (that has never actually served your best interest)? Do you have to explore the depth of your creativity? Do you have to manage your commitments with a reduced income?

Whatever the change may be, find the one thing you can gain from it and do it without any procrastination. It may be tough in the initial stages. You may question your capabilities. Your confidence level may decrease. Persevere, and you will come through. Be patient with yourself. Adapting to change and making it work for you takes time. Continue loving yourself unconditionally, every step of the way. Never doubt yourself. It will be a matter of time before you reap the rewards of your strategy. You will be rewarded for making change work for you.

- *BE AHEAD OF CHANGE.*

After a few experiences of using change to your advantage, you will be in a stronger position to pre-empt change, be it in your career or personal life. Push yourself out of your comfort zone, not because you're competing with someone, but because you're competing with yourself now to become better in the future. Make your endeavours all about personal development. Do you want to work on a professional website to sell your skills online? Do you want to conduct an online workshop on your present expertise? If so, what skills would you need to acquire before your venture? Do you want to double down on expanding your portfolio? What are the changes you can choose to invest in now so that you reap the returns in the future?

Some changes will be unexpected. Others can be pre-empted. You need to think seriously about the changes you want to make in your life. Constantly work towards these changes. You're actually working to fulfil your desires. Be proactive. You will then minimise the occurrence of rude shock. You will then be ahead of change whenever and wherever possible.

- *USE CHANGE TO GET RID OF CLUTTER IN YOUR LIFE.*

However small or big a change, use it as the perfect excuse to make your life clutter-free. I'm talking about things, people, relationships, situations, finances, investments, extra-curricular activities, extra-curricular memberships, etc. The list goes on! These forms of clutter may not have anything to do with the change you're facing. You're just making the most of it to clean up every other aspect of your life. Why not?! What better time to make additional changes? By doing so, you're freeing up your mind, space, and energy for positivity and abundance to flow into your life continuously. Use change to make major changes. Use change to transform yourself and your life for the better. Any kind of clutter will hinder your progress. It will pollute your mind and adversely affect your well-being. It could even compromise your health. If change did not strike, you could be living a life full of clutter for many more years. This may sound dramatic, but it's the bitter truth. Use change as a catalyst to cleanse your soul and remove all negativity and toxicity from your life. With this as a motive, how could you possibly refuse to embrace change?

Understand and know that change is a blessing for you to rediscover yourself. You need change. Accept change as you would accept your friend. Use change as an opportunity to reach for your highest potential. Use change as an indispensable tool to equip yourself with skills and knowledge that propel you to prosperity. Work with change to create peace, stability and happiness in your life – mentally, emotionally and spiritually.

BY LETTING GO, YOU'RE LETTING THE UNIVERSE WORK ITS MAGIC FOR YOU. DON'T MISTAKE IT FOR GIVING UP! – MEERA JHOGASUNDRAM

Chapter Six

LIVE YOUR DREAM

What are your dreams? I'm not talking about the dreams you wish for, knowing that you have no intention of pursuing them. I'm talking about your dreams of the kind of life you'd like to live in this lifetime. Don't have any yet? Let me help you. What would you like to do on a daily basis for the rest of your life? What kind of environment would you like to live in long term? What kind of people would like to be surrounded by? Are you more of an introvert or an extrovert? What does success mean to you? What does abundance mean to you? What do you believe in the most? What inspires and encourages your creativity? What gives rise to peace and calmness within you? These questions may ignite the suppressed passions longing for expression.

Your authentic dream is usually the one that you never share completely with anyone. It symbolises deep-rooted desires kept hidden within you for a long time. Perhaps you've shared bits and pieces of your dream with a few people closest to you. I believe that no one but you knows exactly what your deepest desires are. There will always be a big part of your dream that you choose not to share with anyone. It's too personal. It means too much to you. You're certainly not going to give anyone an opportunity to judge it or judge you.

When you pursue your dream, expect to encounter hypocrisy, jealousy and criticism. Expect to be judged in one way or another. Don't expect people to understand. Distance yourself from nay-sayers.

I'm not being a pessimist. I'm being realistic. There are all kinds of people on this planet. You cannot possibly please everyone. You've got to understand and accept that you have absolutely no control over other people's beliefs, thoughts and actions. Know that they're just being themselves. That should not have any impact on you. You are different. You are unique. Your dream is unique to you. Only you can fully understand how much your dream means to you.

Don't bother justifying the actions you take to live your best life. You could explain your choices to those who matter to you. Even if they fail to understand, it shouldn't deter you or dampen your spirit. When you break free from tradition, cultural behaviour, societal expectations and constraints, generational practices, or religious beliefs, expect resistance and even a backlash. Be prepared for it. There's no point in asking questions such as why don't they understand? How can they be so judgemental? Why are they thinking less of me? Why do they think that I'm a failure? These queries will get you nowhere.

I want to stress that I'm in no way encouraging you to break free from anything in particular. I'm merely asking you to be true to yourself so that you can live a meaningful and fulfilling life. If you decide that it's best for you to break free from what you perceive to be self-limiting beliefs, I'm asking you to stick to your decision, come what may. Why? Because you are worth it. Because you deserve to live life your way. The prerequisite is that you have carefully thought things through and you're willing and prepared to take full responsibility for your actions, as well as the consequences. Yes, in other words, it's time to grow up!

I gave the concept of 'living my dream' serious thought only about a year before I wrote this book. Before that, I was too consumed by what I thought was my dream. That old dream was founded on false beliefs and superficial expectations. I realised this while living in Geneva, pursuing my doctorate. I had a terrifying realisation. I discovered my truth that the qualification I was striving for had absolutely nothing to do with any aspect of my true dream. I cannot begin to describe the intensity of resistance within me. For some time, I wasn't sure what to do. I was lost. I lost interest in my thesis.

I was feeling trapped. I desperately tried to find ways to motivate myself to get back to my thesis, but I failed miserably. My days were gloomy. My nights were scary. I didn't know what I was going to do for a living. I knew that it was not going to be anything related to my thesis. I spent many days and months walking around my apartment, not feeling like doing anything. I made frequent trips to Lake Geneva where I spent many hours with the swans, seagulls, ducks, pigeons and other birds. I felt hopeless. I felt as though I was being suffocated by all the void within me.

I didn't understand what was happening to me, within me. How is it possible that prior to this, throughout my working life, I was always ambitious, constantly upgrading my skills? I completed one degree after another. As if that wasn't enough, I also completed a diploma course on employment relations. You can imagine how exhausting and demanding that must have been. I was working full time and pursuing my studies part time. I was worn out. I often experienced burnouts. I never travelled abroad for the holidays because I was saving my vacation leave to study for exams. Yet I never complained.

In my mind, I knew what I was working for: career advancement. I truly believed that my qualifications would enable me to live my dream. I never gave a thought to what my dream actually might be. I chose to believe that my life purpose was to do my best in my job at that time, to go as far as I could professionally, earn a comfortable salary, and live a life of abundance. I never questioned any of these. I never second-guessed myself. I just blindly worked towards achieving these goals.

I'm not sure what the underlying reasons were for these supposed desires. I'm not sure how I developed such desires. I never doubted that they were actually my desires. I just went all out bettering myself and improving my life. So I thought. I never stopped to think if any of these goals made me happy. I just bulldozed my way through achievements, one after another. I wanted a positive change. I assumed that change was career advancement in the organisation that I worked for so many years. In other words, my goals, dreams and ambition were defined and constrained by where I worked. Why did I allow this? I really don't know.

Now, when I look back, I realise that it could be because I was living my life on autopilot mode. It could be because I attached my worth to my achievements and the salary I was earning at that point. It could be because of the society in which I was raised and educated. It could be because I never explored any other option due to the self-limiting belief that my life is meant to be lived only in this way. Perhaps external expectations had seeped into my subconscious mind, dictating the decisions I made. Perhaps I was too afraid to step out of my comfort zone and do something completely different. Perhaps I didn't respect myself enough to give myself a chance to find out what I truly wanted to do for the rest of my life.

At this juncture, I feel the need to divulge and write about my involvement in the performing arts. For a good ten years of my life, I was actively teaching and performing Bharatanatyam, an Indian classical dance form. I was part of a non-profit performing arts company that was putting up numerous shows locally and abroad. Apart from work and sleep, all my time was spent training and performing. This period of time was before I chose the path of academic excellence to further my career. I was younger, full of energy, passionate about expressing myself through dance, and hoping for an opportunity to become a full-time professional performing artiste. I was also a dance choreographer for various national events and for students doing their debut performances. I simply loved expressing myself through dance. At that point in my life, it was my identity.

Work was sustenance and dance was an opportunity for me to thrive. What I didn't realise was that I was actually short-changing myself. I've always been academically inclined, but I dismissed that ability of mine for those ten years because I was so afraid that I would have to give up my dream of becoming a professional performing artiste. I have to admit that my intuition was frequently reminding me of all the other things in life that I might be interested in. I dismissed it. My mind was set on dance and nothing else.

Towards the tail end of that ten-year period, something strange happened. The joy and satisfaction that I derived from dance was fast declining. Each performance became a chore instead of an opportunity. Due to frequent training sessions, I found myself always in a state of physical exhaustion. This greatly impacted my mental, emotional, and spiritual well-being. I realise now that I pushed myself too hard in my passion. Everything has a limit, and I crossed mine. Handling a full-time job and all my dance commitments became more and more challenging. I began feeling resentful. That was a very sad experience because I loved to dance.

I tried to break things apart so that I could fully understand why I was feeling so negative about my passion. I reasoned out that I loved dancing during training sessions, but performing was too taxing for me, given my other commitments. I realised that the frequency of performances was too demanding for me, personally, given my full-time job. I was getting older, and my stamina was going down. Meaning, I had to practise more and harder to deliver the same standard of performance as before. This is by no means a valid excuse. I don't want to give the impression that I'm making excuses. As an individual, I couldn't keep up with the demands of all my commitments equally. I had to prioritise.

The desire to further my studies was getting stronger. I wanted to explore other interests. I felt that my passion was restricting my life. I want to make it clear that this was my personal experience. In no way should this be generalised. In no way should it compromise the art of dance itself. I realised that I wasn't prepared to live with the uncertainties that would dominate my life as a full-time performing artiste, if I chose that path, especially in my social setting. I realised that I wanted something more, though I didn't quite know what it was that I was so desperately seeking. I realised that my time in Indian classical dance was well spent, and at that point, after about a decade, it was over. I have no regrets. I am grateful for the wealth of experience that I had acquired. I am grateful for the exposure to different cultures, audiences and creative projects. My involvement in dance was pivotal in stimulating my creativity and anchoring my confidence. For this reason, I will always be grateful!

I was astonished at my change of heart. I didn't expect to stop performing. Yet I chose to do it. It was my free will. This shift within led me to believe that my future was in the pursuit of academic excellence and climbing the corporate ladder. This is why I was so determined to see how far I could push myself forward professionally in my work organisation. I believe you'll have a clearer picture now about why I persevered in advancing my career despite the fact that my immediate work environment was pure toxicity. Even at that turning point, I never stopped to think what truly ignited the fire within me. I never gave myself the chance to explore other options. Shocking but true.

Getting back to my PhD student life, I did achieve what I aimed for. As I mentioned earlier, I was offered a doctoral candidature in Geneva, during which I lost interest in my thesis topic. Another unexplainable shock! I've always understood myself to be a go-getter, which made it difficult for me to figure out why I was so detached from my thesis. After a substantial amount of time spent doing nothing productive with regard to my studies, I finally admitted to myself that I've always had a flair for writing. I've always been passionate about improving myself, motivating myself. That's how I reached this far. No one had to push me. No one had to help me. I did it all by myself. Personal growth and development have always dominated my choices in life, be it in dance or at the workplace. I've always been passionate about becoming my best self and living at my highest potential. My intensive involvement in the performing arts and my relentless pursuit of academic excellence tied to career advancement is the proof in the pudding.

Motivation, self-empowerment and personal development were the areas I've always been passionate about. While writing my thesis in Geneva, I also rediscovered my love for animals and the environment. Climate change issues triggered troubling questions within me. Environmental justice, wildlife conservation, and ocean conservation became passion projects in social media. I would post daily on one or more of these issues, in addition to posting inspiring content on self-improvement. I started a YouTube channel posting weekly motivational videos. I began answering lots of questions on Quora relating to personal development. I began posting content daily on multiple social media platforms such as Twitter, Facebook, Pinterest, LinkedIn and my personal website. I looked forward to these activities. It was time consuming and mentally exhausting. Still, I thoroughly enjoyed it.

Soon after I started my YouTube channel, the desire to write a non-fiction book helping people to live their best lives arose within me. I wanted to keep my YouTube content alive. I was so motivated to write about my take on motivation. I was inspired to share my journey on self-empowerment. I wanted to create something that would help people. I wanted to make a positive difference in their lives. More importantly, I wanted this to be an ongoing process. I wanted to share my experiences so that others could avoid making similar compromised choices. I was beginning to live my best life, and I was excited to help others become their best selves. My aim is to empower as many people as I possibly can, especially the youth. You are my most valued witness on this beautiful journey. Why? Because you've joined me from the very beginning. After reading my first book, I trust that you'll join me on my subsequent ventures.

The realisations and epiphanies came on gradually. It wasn't one moment or one day. But after a period of time, when I looked back, the amazing journey of self-realisation became apparent to me. I was overwhelmed with gratitude and joy. I shed happy tears. I had finally discovered my passions. I had finally discovered the direction in which I was heading. I was scared of failing. At the same time, I was overjoyed and driven to give it my all!

There's something I want to highlight. I learned not to define the path to my dream. Meaning, once I begin the journey to my dream, I am prepared for changes. While I have a plan and expectations of how to achieve my dream, my strategy is fluid and always open to changes. I'm talking about changes that are far better than my original plan of action; changes that will enable me to reach my goal more efficiently and effectively. I am open to new ways of thinking, new approaches. I am open to learning new skills and trying new things to keep up with changing times. I am always willing to step out of my comfort zone, no matter how strong the resistance is within me. I know very well that far more important than the destination is the experience lived during the journey.

There is something that I want you to be prepared for while pursuing your dreams. By now you would have realised that dreams change or evolve at different stages in your life. You have childhood dreams and teenage dreams. They could be completely unrelated. You have dreams in your twenties. When you reach your thirties, they either transform into something else or you're just no longer passionate about them. Priorities change. Preferences and tastes change. Along with these, desires and goals change. Therefore, dreams are bound to change. Don't be rigid and stick to a vision that you had about a decade ago simply because you're too afraid to dream bigger or dream something new.

One more thing…dreams can evolve along the way. Be prepared to dream more and dream bigger. Don't restrict yourself to one particular vision. For instance, once you achieve your dream, it's highly unlikely that you'll remain stagnant at that spot. You'll probably want more from that dream or you'll build on it and desire something else. This is a fact of life. Desire keeps us going. Just be sure that you're always in control of your desires and not vice versa. Otherwise, you risk falling into the trap of obsession. There's another possibility that could play out. While pursuing your dream, you may stumble upon a bigger vision that encompasses your initial goal. Don't be intimidated by it. Don't let fear and doubt get in the way. If you really want it, I mean if you badly want it, you owe it to yourself to give it your best shot. Don't short-change yourself by resisting it.

Be true to yourself, honest with yourself at all times, no compromises. It's your responsibility to make sure that your dream is defined by you alone, whatever point you're at in your journey. If your dream has changed, acknowledge it, admit it, accept it, and start working towards it. There's no point in pondering over the time wasted on an old dream. There's no use trying to figure out why your dream has changed. Don't impede your own growth. Don't be delayed by things that no longer matter. Don't waste your time on anything that doesn't serve your present vision. Always remember, there's a reason for your change of heart. Honour it.

Expect and be prepared for your dreams to change and evolve throughout your life. Accept new dreams without judging yourself. Understand and know that you are worthy of your desires. You know my story about horse riding. You know my story about the performing arts. You know my story about career advancement. I'll let you in on something else. I love playing the piano. I love classical music. I went for classical piano lessons for at least six years. Reprogramming the way my brain worked was tough. I was an adult beginner. Despite the challenges, I persevered until I moved to Geneva for my studies.

My commitments took priority, and playing the piano was pushed to the back of my mind. It has been several years now since I've played the piano. I still love playing the instrument. But for now, I have stopped pursuing my dream of going all the way in that area. Why? I was writing my thesis while being totally confused about what I actually wanted to do for the rest of my life. As I've discovered what my path is, all my energy and attention is continuously being channelled in that direction. You've come this far reading my book. You know what my current path is. Once again, I'd like to stress that the future is pretty much a mystery to me. I am excited about it. I am curious to see how events unfold in my life and whether I'll be able to include piano lessons in my life again. One of the most precious lessons I've learned – always be open to change!

My dream of becoming a full-time performing artiste changed. My dream of excelling in horse riding changed. My dream of climbing the corporate ladder changed. My dream of working in a job related to my thesis changed. This is why I made it clear in previous chapters that though I know for sure what I love doing now, I cannot be sure that

I will not branch off into something else in the future. Let me put it this way. Whatever brings out the best in me, whatever allows me to reach my highest potential, whatever ignites my passion and sparks my creativity, whatever feeds my soul and eventually my pocket, whatever gives me a sense of fulfilment and achievement, whatever gives me joy, whatever makes me feel that I'm contributing to our planet and mankind in a significant way, whatever makes me feel closest to nature and the animals that I love so dearly – that is my dream!

What a broad range of possibilities! That's precisely what I've learned through my experiences. I've learned to always keep an open mind and accept changes. Life has taught me that until I try something for myself, I will never know how well I would have fared in that area. I am prepared for new dreams. I am excited about all that life has in store for me. I am thrilled because I don't see what's in the distant future, yet I'm loving every moment of all that I'm doing presently. Most importantly, I am so grateful that I feel and think this way. I am so grateful that I've broken free from self-limiting beliefs. I am so grateful for the opportunity to have new dreams.

Whatever your dream is, just make sure you're true to yourself and always be open to changes. Be prepared for your dreams to change, especially when you enter a new phase in life. My lessons are not tailored to your specific situation. But I have four solid suggestions that will help you throughout your life.

1. LIVE IN THE MOMENT

It's important to have a dream. It's important to visualise details of your dream life. It's important to plan and work towards your dream. You must be thinking – so how do I think about the future, plan for it and live in the moment all at the same time? It's a fair question. My questions for you – How do you think your life would be if you had no dream? Do you think you'd be motivated? How would you feel if you had nothing significant to look forward to? Indeed, it would be a mundane existence!

Your dream is a reflection of your life purpose. It symbolises your contribution to our planet and humanity. It gives you a reason to do your best, to strive for better. Believe it or not, your dream actually helps you live in the moment. How is this possible? Let me explain.

The journey to realising your dream will teach you many invaluable life lessons. It will probably be similar to a ride on a roller coaster. It has to be. How else are you going to gain the strength to fight for what you love? How else are you going to gain the courage to unapologetically enjoy what you love? You need to be moulded into the perfect cogwheel fit for your dream. Living in the moment prepares you for your dream. When you cherish every moment of life, not only the energy flowing through you but also all forms of life around you, you'll realise how precious being alive is. You'll realise that you need very little to lead an abundant life. You'll realise that wealth is an inside job. You'll become more appreciative. You'll become more grateful. You'll become more and more prepared to live your dream.

What can you do to live in the moment?

- ***Do everything in your life consciously.***

I want to stress that being alive does not necessarily mean that you're living consciously. It's so easy to do your daily routine without paying attention to it. Think about these questions: When you brush your teeth, are you thinking about that meeting at work or is your attention on every tooth that is still in good health? When you're making your favourite cup of coffee, are you thinking about the groceries you need for the week or are you taking in the stimulating aroma of your day-starter and being thankful for it? Do you gulp down your morning drink or do you savour every sip? When you walk to the train station or your car, do you pay attention to activities around you or are you engrossed in thoughts about something that's not working out the way you expected? Do you consciously listen to the birds chirping or do you dismiss it as noise? When you're carrying your grocery bags home, are you dreading it as a chore or being grateful that you have the strength to do things for yourself independently? When you cook a meal for yourself, are you observing how healthy and beautiful the tomatoes look as you slice them, or are you thinking about that meal at the restaurant that you'd rather have? Be absolutely honest with yourself. All of us are guilty of doing things on autopilot mode. Some are guilty of living their life on autopilot mode. I hope you're not one of them. It's important to dream and plan for your future. At the same time, you've got to prioritise every living moment, every breath you take. The sooner you understand that the next moment and the next breath is not guaranteed, the better you'll appreciate being present.

This may sound ridiculous, especially if you're new to this way of living. Begin with small steps. When you wake up every morning, before you get out of bed, be conscious of the fact that you're alive and you have the opportunity of another day. It's very similar to living in gratitude. You can't possibly live in the moment and not be grateful for it. Both go hand in hand. When you're watching a movie, please don't read your mail or send text messages. If the movie is boring, watch something else that interests you. Your attention is best focused on the one thing that you're doing in the moment. Often that's how great ideas are born. Your mind is channelled in one direction and free to be triggered in creative ways by whatever you're doing. Let me explain. Your undivided attention is on those potatoes and tomatoes you're slicing when suddenly a solution to a long-standing problem sprouts in your mind. You could be doing just about anything consciously and mindfully when you experience such aha moments. It's such a great feeling!

Please don't practise being present expecting solutions to problems. Let it happen spontaneously. Let it happen naturally. Let the Universe surprise you. It's a reward for being present while doing your thing.

- *SPEND TIME WITH THE EXPERTS.*

I believe at some point in your life, you would have had the privilege of spending time with or around those who have been, are, and will always be the experts on living in the moment. If you have pets, you know exactly what I'm talking about. If you don't, there are still other options. Do you live in a place where you have access to animals? Are there birds, ducks, geese, and swans in a park or botanical garden near your residence? Do you think you can schedule visits to the zoo or an animal shelter every other month? The simplest way to be around these experts would be to find some spot, preferably in nature, where you can sit undisturbed for at least thirty minutes. You're bound to come across a sparrow, pigeon or some other bird. What I'm trying to get at is you're unlikely to be completely deprived of this privilege.

When you're around animals, observe them. Look at their behaviour throughout your thirty minutes. That will happen naturally. You'll be so intrigued just watching them live in the moment. They are also experts in living from moment to moment. They are totally aware of their environment. They're acutely aware of possible danger. They're completely in tune with their instincts and everything that happens in their immediate surrounding. They know how to seize every moment and live life to the fullest. They know that the next moment is not guaranteed. They don't procrastinate or postpone because they're busy doing their best to get through that moment, to get through that day.

Are you doing that or are you overwhelmed and discouraged thinking about all that you have to do in the future? When you observe animals, they know they're being watched, yet they are fully focused on doing what's best for them in that moment. Can you do that for yourself? Don't try. Just do it. Do you now know why it's so fascinating to watch these experts in action? You may call it survival instincts. I choose to call it passion for life. They are just living without any expectations of themselves or those around them. If a kind soul brings food for them, they seize the opportunity. If not, they look for it elsewhere. They don't judge themselves. They know that they're enough just being in their element.

Spend as much time as you want with the experts. Learn from them. Approach life with the lessons learned and you will discover how magical and miraculous your existence is. This is best experienced and felt. No amount of description does justice to it. Remember to make this a regular practice. As much as your body needs to be fed, your soul craves nourishment.

- ***Spend time in silence.***

Whether you're an introvert, extrovert, or somewhere in between, you need to ground your thoughts and feelings on a daily basis. This will ensure that you make the best of every moment and every breath you take. Otherwise, you risk being whisked away into the black hole of triggered negative thoughts and emotional imbalances. You need to balance your mind, body and soul every day – once in the morning when you wake up, once in the middle of the day, and once before you go to bed.

It would be ideal if you could do some sort of meditation that you're comfortable with. I know that many are sceptical and never actually get down to doing it. Let me make it simple for you. In the morning, before you begin your routine, spend ten minutes in silence without responding to your electronic devices. Close your eyes, sit in a comfortable position on the floor or on a chair, and just make sure you don't think about anything. You'll get the hang of it after some time. When you do it the right way, you'll become so relaxed that at the end of ten minutes you will be close to sleeping. Of course, please don't go back to bed. It defeats the purpose of this exercise. Do the same thing midday and just before you go to bed. The trick is not to think about anything in those ten minutes. Fill your mind with void. Let it be blank.

This is as simple as I can get. Over a period of time, you'll begin to place more value on this 'me' time in silence. You won't be able to put your finger on it. You'll just feel much better and do better throughout your day. It will make you more conscious of your existence. It will make you more mindful of your breathing. You will know that no matter what happens, you can always make peace with yourself. You will know that whatever happens within you is given due care and attention and is well taken care of. When your inner being is fine, you'll be able to go about your day doing whatever needs to be done and being present. You will not be in conflict with yourself or your external environment. You can focus on every moment. You'll be mindful of every breath you take. This will become second nature.

When you become better and more comfortable with silence, you could perhaps progress to taking long, deep breaths. You could extend the duration of this process to fifteen or twenty minutes. You decide what's best for you. You decide what works for you. In the future, you may even want to take it up a notch by attending a relevant class, session or workshop. For someone who's new to this practice, ten minutes of 'me' time in silence three times a day will empower you to begin living in the moment.

I'm going to elaborate a little more in case you're still doubtful. When you understand the value of life, you'll understand how fortunate you are. You'll want to make the most of the time you have on this planet. You will not have the time nor the patience to put up with society's fluff and façade. You'll know that time is running out. You'll realise that there are so many more things that you want to do, goals that you want to achieve, and places that you want to visit. You'll be motivated to take inspired action. You'll want to take the best route to your dream. 'He said', 'she said', and 'they said' will no longer matter. You'll know that ultimately your desires matter most. I believe you have a clearer picture now.

2. LIVE YOUR DREAM YOUR WAY

You know what your dream is. You know what you need to do to achieve it. You're taking action, and that's great! There will be well-wishers offering you advice. There will be friends offering suggestions. There will be family members offering help. It's important to ask for help when you need it. No one is an island. No one can survive and thrive alone. We need one another to exist. At the same time, you've got to understand that you are complete within yourself. All the answers you seek are within you. The guidance you seek speaks to you all the time through your intuition. Be self-reliant and only ask for help when you're unable to manage on your own. In the long run, you'll be appreciated for this.

Your thinking process, your preferences, your character and personality, and your tolerance level for different things are unique to you. You know best how much you're willing to compromise and what you're willing to compromise. You know best what's a 'want' and what's a 'need' for you. You know yourself best. When you ask for help that you don't really need, you may be overwhelmed with advice, suggestions and instructions. You may end up feeling confused. You may not eventually decide on the best option for you because you don't want to offend someone who matters to you. This is what I call unnecessary compromise.

Take charge of the situation. Do what's best for you. Do it your way. If you need help, by all means ask for it. Make it clear that there are no strings attached and that you'll be the one making the final decision. That way, misunderstandings will be minimised. You won't risk offending anyone. People who care about you and respect you will understand where you're coming from. They'll be convinced that you know exactly what you're doing. They'll know that you're not fickle or undecided. They'll know that you don't need much help.

Why is it so important to live your way? Because it ensures that you take responsibility for your actions. It ensures that you are accountable for your choices. You will then be motivated to do everything in your power to make sure that you succeed in living your dream. There's no room for any excuse. The way you live your life, the decisions you make on a daily basis, the friendships you grow to rely on more – all these will align with you when you take charge of your situation, take charge of yourself, and thus take charge of your life.

3. TURN OBSTACLES INTO OPPORTUNITIES

You're on the path to living your dream. You're doing things your way. Expect obstacles along the way. I don't mean to be a wet blanket. I just don't want you to be caught off-guard. It's not realistic to think that it's going to be a smooth-sailing journey. Hurdles appear before you to keep you on your toes. Otherwise, you risk becoming complacent. In each obstacle lies a hidden opportunity. It's your job to discover what that is. This is the process through which you grow, evolve and transform. Every obstacle is a test. You have free will to choose to pass or fail. If you succumb to challenges, you won't be able to move forward in the best way possible. You may or may not achieve your dream. You may manage to live your dream for a while, but it will not last.

Learn every lesson so well that you don't have to repeat it. These experiences prepare you for your ultimate dream. A lesson not learned will repeat itself. Why slow down your growth? Why delay your dream? When you've overcome all the obstacles on your path, you'll be sending the Universe a crucial message – 'I'm ready to receive. I'm ready for my dream!' Remember, be it positive or negative, every experience in your life is a necessary one. There is a purpose for it. There is a lesson you need to learn from it. Nothing you have been through, nothing you are going through, and nothing you will go through in the future is going to be wasted. I can't wait for you to reach the point in your life when you realise this. Know that nothing is going to happen until or unless you're ready. The good news is that you've already been given the heads up on this. You're reading this aren't you?

One step at a time. One obstacle at a time. One dream at a time. What do I mean by this? Human nature will always desire more. When you start living your dream, you're bound to have another dream, and then another, and then another. It goes on until your last breath. At the end of your journey, I believe you'll want to look back on a life well-lived, rich in experiences and preferably with no regrets. Most importantly, you'll want to look back on a life abundant and deep-rooted in love. For this, you've got to love yourself unconditionally first. Without this, you can't move forward. You'll be stuck. I can't stress this enough!

4. GET USED TO HANDLING TOXIC PEOPLE

I went through a mind battle deciding where to put this section. Handling toxic people can fit into any one of my seven chapters. I finally decided to include it here because living your dream encompasses everything that I talked about. So does dealing with toxic people. They are all around our planet. For instance, people who support and encourage racism; people who intentionally spread fake news; climate deniers who continue to claim that the adverse effects of climate change are a hoax; people in your social circle who occupy their days judging you by their superficial standards; relatives who, for reasons best known to them, choose to focus on your life over their own; colleagues who plot, plan and conspire to bring you down, fuelled by their jealousy and insecurities. And the list goes on.

Toxic people are everywhere. They will continue to be everywhere. This is a harsh reality. The sooner you face it, the better you can deal with it in a way that results in an outcome that's best for you. I'm sure you have had your fair share of experiences with toxic people. When you're in a situation where you have to work with them, the toxicity can be quite contagious. At the very least, you will have to hear what they have to say, often about others. Their negativity could extend to you if you're blatantly hostile. You may have to silently put up with senseless criticisms and gossip just to get the work done, sometimes even to prove that you're a team player. I've just scratched the surface. There's so much negativity that could stick to you in the long run without you even realising it when you're in contact with toxic people for prolonged periods of time.

You would have gleaned some idea of this from descriptions of my work environment in previous chapters. I could go on for days as I have decades of experience in this area. My intention is to help you as best as I can to manoeuvre your way through these tricky people. Know that you will be coming across people displaying different levels of toxic behaviour throughout your lifetime. Don't be shocked when it happens. Be prepared.

- Firstly, when you're surrounded by toxic people, make sure your focus is entirely on yourself. Make sure that you're always working on your progress. What skills would you like to upgrade? Take action. Don't even think of getting their opinion or letting them know. You don't owe any of them an explanation. What courses would you like to attend to further your career? Have you applied for them? Take action. Are you academically inclined? If so, have you thought about how you can move forward in your path to academic excellence? Have you figured out something? Do you have a plan? Take action. What else do you need to do to step up your personal and professional development? Are you doing it or are you procrastinating? Take action. What kind of legacy would you like to leave behind for future generations? How would you like to help people, even when you're no longer on this planet?

Think about all these questions and more. Think about your life, your well-being, your ambition. Think about all that you want to do for the rest of your days. Give it your undivided attention. Be so engrossed in working on yourself that any toxic distraction and negativity aimed at you would just dissipate. You will be fully occupied with improving yourself and working towards your bright future. You will not have time for anything that doesn't add value to your life.

- Secondly, distance yourself from toxic people and situations. If possible, completely avoid them. But how do you avoid them when you're working with them? Don't fall into the trap of being labelled as 'anti-social'. Do your part and be sure not to participate in any gossip or conspiracy. Be sure not to malign anyone just because the toxic team you're in thrives on doing that. Use your discretion. Always maintain your dignity and integrity.

After doing your best, if you find that things are getting worse and your peace of mind is greatly compromised, don't wait for a miracle that will never happen. Create your own miracle by exploring all your options. Perhaps you could apply for a transfer to another department. Perhaps you could apply for another position elsewhere. Perhaps you could work towards self-employment. If you keep an

YOU ARE THE KEY

open mind, the options are limitless. Remember, you are worthy, and you deserve the best.

How do you avoid toxic relatives? This could prove to be especially challenging. There will always be family functions, birthdays, anniversaries, festivals, holidays, etc. You've got to be smart and tactful. Cut down socialising with them. Cut down communicating with them. During get-together celebrations, always be busy doing something or talking to someone. This way, you'll minimise interaction with them. Do this gradually over a long period of time. You may be accused of being snobbish. You may be accused of being cold and unfriendly. Don't take it to heart. Don't place any value on frivolous comments. You know who you are and why you're doing it. That's what matters most. You're always going to be the best person to look out for yourself. It is so important for you to understand that absolutely nothing is worth compromising your sanity.

If you're in a toxic relationship…well, I don't even know why you would continue to short-change yourself by choosing to continue to be in such a relationship. You are not as helpless as you think you are. You always have a choice, whether or not you acknowledge it. I can't decide for you, but I can ask you – why not choose your well-being? Why not choose to get out of that toxic relationship? Why not choose yourself first?

- Thirdly, be prepared and expect to deal with toxic people throughout your life. The distancing and avoiding will work in some situations, not all the time. I'm not being a pessimist. I'm being realistic. Let me explain. Let's say you've left a job that was surrounded by negative, toxic people. When you begin working in a new environment, expect to encounter toxic people. Why? Because there will always be people who love to gossip, who are jealous of something that you have, who are insecure, who are too lazy to work on themselves but not lazy enough to not mind your business. These are human traits that have thrived in humankind since time immemorial. As long as humans exist, it's not possible to eradicate these behaviours.

I cannot stress this enough. There is a reason for your desires and dreams. That reason is unique to you. It is tied to the purpose of your existence. Don't trivialise it. Don't dismiss it. Don't allow external influence and interference to deter you. Be honest with yourself. Don't justify, apologise or feel guilty for choosing your dream over others' expectations of you. Your life is a gift and opportunity for you to live your dream. Always cherish your gift. Always honour your desire.

WHEN YOU HAVE THE COURAGE TO LIVE YOUR DREAM, THE UNIVERSE CONSPIRES TO PAVE THE WAY FOR YOU. – MEERA JHOGASUNDRAM

Chapter Seven

Give Back to Our Planet

Y ou've begun building the foundation for living your best life. You're focused on living your dream. You know that it's going to take time to reach your destination. You also know that you're on the right track – the path meant for you. You're feeling confident, motivated and inspired. You're not afraid of the hard work you have to put in to realise your dreams. You've got that spark back. Though you don't know how things are going to materialise, you just know that they're going to work out for you. You know this because you've started believing in yourself. You're feeling good about yourself. You know and accept that you're amazing, despite your shortcomings. You understand that there is only one you. You're owning your uniqueness.

I understand how you're feeling. I love that you've come this far. More importantly, I want you to keep going forward while maintaining this emotional and mental state of positivity. Of course, you'll come across challenges. You may not feel the peak of happiness every moment. Life's peaks and valleys can sometimes take you on an emotional roller coaster. That's OK. You're human. Give yourself permission to go down when there's a need. But equip yourself to spring back into positivity, because that's where you want to be most of the time. If you've taken up all my suggestions so far, you'll be in a great place.

There is something that you can do to remain in this great place, no matter what life throws at you. There's a way to feel good and positive about yourself, regardless of what happens in your life. There's a way to balance your thoughts, feelings and emotions. There's a way to ground yourself in reality and always live in gratitude. There's a way to appreciate every little pleasure in life, no matter how small it may be.

You've got to find your way of giving back to our planet. What do I mean by this? Understand that there is no standard way of appreciating the environment we live in and the people around us. Why is this so important when you're already living a great life? Because whether or not you realise it, you're not separate from nature and our planet. You're part of it. You're made of nature's elements. By doing something to help our planet thrive, you're practising mindfulness. You're telling the Universe that you're not taking anything in life for granted. You're showing the Creator how grateful you are to be on this planet. You're living consciously. When you live consciously, you automatically make better choices for yourself, the environment in which you live, and thus, our planet.

How can you give back? For starters, ask yourself, what is the issue that's closest to your heart? What change in your environment would make you feel better? The answer could involve human beings, animals, nature, wildlife, or just about anything on our planet. Get involved. Get active. Do your part. You may want to support a cause such as wildlife conservation by donating or by volunteering your services. You may wish to use your expertise and influence on social media to increase awareness on the adverse impact of climate change. You may want to donate money, clothes or food supplies to refugees. You could do something as simple as feeding animals that you come across on your way to work – stray dogs, cats and birds. It all depends on what you strongly believe in standing up for.

There are so many non-profit organisations working hard for multiple causes. You just have to decide on something that calls out to you, something that's very close to your heart. I'll share my experience with you. I derive so much joy from feeding birds. I feed all kinds of birds – swans, seagulls, ducks, mallards, geese, crows, etc. I especially love feeding pigeons and sparrows. To me, they are totally adorable! I've spent enough time with them to know that they possess a very shrewd kind of intelligence. They know and sense your love for them. They demand to be fed. They're not shy about it. If you ask me for proof, well, I have none. It's a gut instinct, perhaps very much like the ones they possess. I cannot describe the feeling of being fulfilled when I feed birds. Watching them savour and cherish every morsel gives me so much satisfaction. My day is made just by doing this. After a feeding session, I'm as happy as I can possibly be.

Another way to explore your creativity and make an impact simultaneously is to build your tribe on social media and promote a social cause that you feel strongly for. You have many options. You'll be spoilt for choices. Organisations fighting for human rights, wildlife conservation, animal welfare, environmental justice, climate action and sustainable living options are active on platforms like Twitter, Instagram, Facebook and YouTube. If you've been using social media for entertainment, relaxation, or even plain gossip, why not expand your horizon? You make a difference to our planet. Believe it. You just have to figure out how you'd like to make a difference. Start posting content that accurately reflects the social cause that you stand for. It doesn't cost you anything. All it takes is your time, creativity and consistency. When you're committed to a cause, any social cause that helps our planet thrive in one way or another, your tribe will align with you in no time. You will build a community of like-minded individuals constantly engaging with one another and you, of course. You could influence and inspire them to do more or to start contributing to society and the environment in whatever way that they're most inclined to. You could increase awareness of troubling trends in the world. When people get together, miracles are made possible.

There is a catch to this. You must have complete faith and conviction in the social cause that you're promoting. It's not about you. It's about the issue you're addressing. People can sense it if you're not fully committed. They are likely to take you less and less seriously with time. So, it's important that you find your best way of delivering your message on a regular basis. Decide on a schedule that works for you and stick to it. Your followers and subscribers will know when they can expect to hear from you. They will rely on you for information. They will keep coming back to you once trust is built.

On your part, you could write, make videos, take photographs or just repost a message that you'd like to share with your online audience. I'm guessing that you'll be inspired to make full use of this opportunity to explore your creativity. Whatever your talent is, find a way to use it to spread your message. You'll love it because you're good at it, and when people start showering you with appreciation, you'll naturally want to do more. It's so important to express your individuality in a creative way. It's food for the soul. It's irreplaceable energy. You'll be functioning at an optimal level. How? As long as you're serving humanity or our planet in some way, you're serving a purpose. Soon, that purpose will serve you. It may lead you to something more that needs your contribution. It may give your life more meaning. It may open doors for you that you never knew existed. A word of caution. When you embark on serving a social cause, don't allow expectations to overwhelm you. Focus on what you believe in, what you enjoy doing, strengthening and expanding your community, and increasing awareness of your message. The rest will fall into place at the right time.

If you're just not interested in any of the issues that I've suggested, it's alright. Perhaps you have a passion for personal development. You could be passionate about interviewing people on this subject and getting different views out in the open. Perhaps you'd like to start a podcast series on self-improvement. These are random suggestions. Find an area of service that ignites your passion. Think seriously about how you'd like to implement it. Garner support from friends and family. Build your community. Promote your messages and increase awareness. Later, you can even consider monetizing your initiative. You've got to understand that there's nothing wrong in thinking along these lines. You have a mission that you're passionate about. You certainly need money for your mission!

I've given you some ideas that you can work on right away. If you'd like to join a non-profit organisation and volunteer your services, go ahead! You could use your skills and talent to promote organisational causes benefitting humanity and our planet at large. There are so many ways of giving back. You've got to go within and discover your truth. Why go through all this trouble? Because you are part of this existence. When our planet thrives, you thrive. Your service will keep you grounded and grateful in other areas of your life. You will understand that everything in this planet is connected. All living things are connected energetically. It's not possible to destroy a part of our planet and expect everything else to be unaffected. Sooner rather than later, destruction will catch up with us.

There is another way in which you can give back to our planet. Vote for responsible leaders who can be held accountable for their actions. I first came across this call to action by the editor of *The Planet* newsletter, policy director at the Environment and Development Resource Centre (EDRC) in Brussels, Dutch environmentalist and former diplomat, Alexander Verbeek, in many of his interviews. Indeed, it is a sound calling! We have witnessed and experienced the ripple effect of voting for irresponsible and fascist leaders throughout the world. In one way or another, this has been detrimental to our planet. Racism, inadequate climate action, climate denial, wildlife destruction, environmental injustice, land degradation, deforestation, and illegal wildlife trade are only a few of the examples of the destruction on our planet due to incompetent and destructive leaders. First, make sure you vote. Don't for a moment think that your vote doesn't count, because it actually makes a world of difference if you make the right choice. Vote for leaders who are committed to saving our planet from further destruction. Vote for leaders who walk the talk. Vote wisely, and you will serve our planet in one of the best ways possible.

Apart from sharing content on climate change, environmental justice, and wildlife conservation on social media, I am also a subscriber of *The Planet* newsletter. This is a platform that specialises in independent journalism and focuses on grave issues related to our planet. It offers sound analyses and just criticisms of policies and practices that have been long overdue for reform. It consistently spreads awareness on environmental justice and the beauty of nature. Through *The Planet,* I am consistently increasing my engagement in environmental issues, and I am constantly in touch with the latest developments. Before you decide on what you would like to do to contribute to our planet's well-being and how you wish to do it, you need to have a clear and objective picture of what actually is going on. Mainstream media often presents predictable information, analyses and opinions. Diverse views are best presented by professional independent writing. I strongly recommend that you subscribe to *The Planet* or any other credible, independent source of journalism to constantly keep yourself abreast of occurrences on our planet. You may even be inspired to do some writing of your own. Don't rule out this possibility.

Second, you will help our planet thrive just by choosing to eat less meat. I'm hoping that you'll eventually realise the cruelty that animals are continuously being subjected to, all day, every day. I'm hoping that you'll eventually develop a strong distaste for consuming meat. I want to highlight that once upon a time, I enjoyed eating meat. I never spared a thought for the livestock that got cruelly treated and transported just so that we could enjoy a meal. Rather, I chose not to think about it. I was too busy trying to do better for myself and better my career. It's truly amazing the way things hit you when you slow down and actually start thinking about things that you've taken for granted all your life.

While delving deeper into environmental issues, I watched the cruelty inflicted on animals by humankind for the sake of humankind. I watched a documentary on how rabbits were skinned alive in a factory in China. I heard the cries of the rabbits. I watched their bodies being mutilated while they suffered every moment. I cried a lot. Tears are rolling down my cheeks as I'm writing this. The cruelty inflicted on rabbits is only one example. I watched much more involving cows, pigs, chickens, dogs, etc. I was deeply troubled. I decided to make a positive change and became a vegetarian. Subsequently, I stopped consuming milk and other dairy products. In the distant past, while actively involved in the performing arts, I was vegetarian for a period of ten years, but it had nothing to do with animal cruelty. When I stopped classical dance training for good, I went back to consuming meat. Clearly, my reasons for abstaining from meat in the past were not strong enough. When you do it for the right reasons, you will come through.

One of the main reasons for deforestation is to facilitate the grazing of livestock that will eventually end up as food for humans. Pandemics are caused by the consumption of certain variations of meat. If people can love dogs, birds, cats and other pets, why aren't they able to show similar compassion towards all animals? Ironic but true. Think about it. Give it some serious thought. You'll be amazed at how your perspective changes when you just stop to think. I'm aware that this is your personal choice. Still, my humble request to you is to choose wisely.

You may not empathise with the issues I've raised. If that's the case, I believe you haven't had the opportunity or time to get more information on these issues. Do yourself a favour. Become more aware of what's happening around you – what's happening in the world, what's happening to our planet. When you know enough, you will begin feeling. You will have an opinion. That's how inspired action is born. Once you figure out the social or environmental cause you strongly identify with, you will align your beliefs, thoughts and actions with it. You will be motivated to support it. I'm hopeful that in your own way, you will take inspired action to help our planet thrive. I'm hopeful that you will choose to serve our planet's needs in some way. I'm hopeful that you will grow to love our planet even more.

You are important. Your service is crucial. Your role in helping our planet thrive is essential. You make a difference. How you wish to make an impact is totally up to you. As much as you need the planet, Mother Earth needs you. Believe it. Act on it. Keep her safe and sound for your future generations. Let this be part of the legacy that you leave behind. Show your gratitude for being able to experience life and nature. Remember, you make a difference!

One of the many ways through which I give back to our planet is writing books that will empower people to live their best lives. I trust that this book will help you in more ways than one. I trust that you will empower yourself to live your dream. I trust that you will find your own unique way of giving back to Mother Earth!

IF YOU WANT TO THRIVE IN LIFE, FIND A WAY TO GIVE BACK TO OUR PLANET. LET IT BE YOUR WAY. WHEN OUR PLANET THRIVES, WE THRIVE. YOU THRIVE! – MEERA JHOGASUNDRAM

Conclusion

BELIEVE THAT IT IS POSSIBLE, AND IT BECOMES A POSSIBILITY. BELIEVE THAT YOU WILL, AND IT BECOMES A CERTAINTY. BELIEVE THAT YOU ARE, AND IT BECOMES YOUR REALITY. – MEERA JHOGASUNDRAM

I am so excited for you. You have successfully completed the first part of this journey with me. There is so much more that you can do for yourself. It's not possible to fit everything into one book. I don't mean to discourage you. My intention is to motivate you to do better and to do more for yourself by taking the first step. Most importantly, it is my wish that you figure out your way of doing what is best for you. You are extremely powerful. You are more powerful than you can ever imagine. Are you willing to tap into your power? Are you willing to face your truth? Are you willing to face your fears, doubts and insecurities and challenge them? Are you willing to put in the effort to empower yourself?

I want you to keep three crucial points in mind at all times:

Nothing you have been through is for nothing. Everything has its own purpose. If you haven't already realised this, you will certainly understand what I mean in time to come.

No matter how bad things get, find the lesson, learn it well, and never forget it.

You have the power to live the life you desire. You just have to make sure that you exercise your will to wield that power.

Life may have been tough. Life may become more challenging. Understand and know that you have complete control only of yourself.

Trying to control outcomes and others' actions and opinions will lead to frustration and disappointment. Don't waste your precious time and energy on futile attempts. Focus on yourself, your progress, and your well-being. Make a conscious effort to stay positive at all times. Tough but not impossible. Never stop believing in yourself. Work towards becoming your own best friend. Work towards accepting and loving yourself unconditionally. When you're calm and stable within, you will be able to face any challenge with strength, fortitude and resolve. There is no winning or losing in life. There is only learning and not learning. If you refuse to learn, you cannot grow. Always be the student who is willing to learn and grow from every experience.

The seven chapters in my book will open doors in your mind and your heart. They will provoke you to re-examine your approach to life. They will empower you to take your first step on your path to self-discovery. They will challenge your self-limiting beliefs and preconceived ideas. They will inspire you to break free from your mental cage. They will motivate you to live the life you desire, not the life others desire for you.

Will you take action to live your best life? Do you have the courage to stand up for what you truly believe in? Will you persevere until you fulfil your dreams? A lot depends on you, my friend. My desire is for you to take some form of positive action to improve your life after reading my book. Be practical. You can't aim to implement all my suggestions at one go. Be patient with yourself. Find a pace that works for you. One improvement at a time. One step at a time. Don't judge yourself. Every time you fall, pick yourself up and take a step forward.

While you're engrossed in your journey to self-discovery, my next book will guide you further along the path, if you allow it. And the next. And the next. That will not be the end. There is no end to self-improvement and personal development. Circumstances change. People change. You and I are no exceptions. My goal is to consistently and continuously motivate, inspire and cheer you on in your endeavours. If you have benefited in any way from my book, I trust that you will enjoy being part of my tribe. I trust that you will always stay connected with me through my work on multiple social media platforms, especially on YouTube and Twitter where the focus is on highlighting themes and concepts from my present and forthcoming books. I trust that you will share your own experiences so that like-minded people may learn from you. I would love to know your take on the content discussed in my book. I would love to know your key takeaways. I would love to know the different ways in which you have taken inspired action.

I want you to understand that personal growth is a lifelong journey. Change is your vehicle. You will grow, evolve and transform at a pace unique to you. Be sure not to make comparisons. When you commit to learning and exploring your potential, you will change. You will grow. How gracefully you grow and how much you grow will determine the quality of your experience on this planet. Give it your best shot. Give it your all. You owe it to yourself to live your best life. You owe it to yourself to do it your way. You owe it to yourself to never stop believing in yourself.

Remember, you are the key that can unlock the life you desire. You are the magician who can make your wishes come true. You are the master who can command your dreams to reality. You are far more powerful than you think you are. Understand it. Believe it. Know it.

When you know you're heading in the right direction, don't be overwhelmed by the 'how'. Take one step at a time. Focus on the 'now', and your 'how' will reveal itself in stages. – Meera Jhogasundram

I look forward to your engagement in the next leg of this journey!

YOUR PATH IS MEANT TO BE WALKED BY YOU. THE SOONER YOU REALISE THAT THERE IS NO PURPOSE IN SEEKING APPROVAL TO LIVE YOUR PURPOSE, THE MORE PURPOSEFUL YOUR LIFE BECOMES. – MEERA JHOGASUNDRAM

Acknowledgements

Firstly, I'd like to thank my family, especially my uncles and aunts for their constant support and encouragement. They have always honoured my choices and motivated me to do my best. They have always believed in me. They have always been proud of my achievements and cheered me on. I would not have come this far without them. They have stood by me through many challenges and they continue to look out for me. For this, I am extremely grateful.

I am so grateful to my friends Annhanim Mohamed, Jasmine Ng, Ann Tan and Kelvin Koo for being supportive through the many years we've known one another and for always believing in me. I always rely on them for raw and honest feedback. I am grateful for their friendship and encouragement.

I'd like to thank my coach, Kerk Murray for his invaluable guidance and my go-to person for publishing this book, Rachael Williams for her support and motivation. These two people from Self-Publishing School have been instrumental in constructing a firm foundation for my author journey. I could not have published this book without their help and the support of the team at Self-Publishing School. I am also grateful for the incredible support of the vibrant community of authors in the school.

I'd like to thank my editor, Sky Nuttall for her amazing guidance through the very crucial editing process. I am extremely grateful to Carly Catt, my outstanding proof-reader who went beyond what was required of her, just to refine my manuscript. I am awestruck by her commitment, initiative and professionalism.

I am filled with gratitude for Joris and his team, Mariska and Nada at Cutting Edge Studio for being the icing on the cake. The sound advice of Joris, the incredibly amazing artistry of Nada in creating the cover design for my book and the excellent formatting skills of Mariska have made this part of my journey nothing but pure pleasure. I am so grateful to the three of them for transforming my vision into an impeccably beautiful reality.

All of you have given me numerous reasons to be grateful. To me, each reason is a blessing. From the bottom of my heart, thank you!

Author Biography

About Meera Jhogasundram

Meera Jhogasundram is a career transition coach, deeply intuitive author, and a PhD candidate in international relations. Driven by her passion help her clients reach their highest potential, she is presently pursuing ICF credentials to enhance her coaching services. She loves exploring the underlying reasons for blocks and challenges one is likely to encounter around self-empowerment and personal development. She is passionate about the subject matter of *You are the key* and all her forthcoming books. She is of the conviction that the individual possesses the power to choose to live at the highest possible potential. Her life experiences and her research in the field of personal growth have motivated her to take inspired action and embark on the empowering journey of helping people through her books.

You are the key is the beginning of a venture, aiming to inspire people to live life to the fullest.

Meera is also a lover of nature and animals. She loves feeding animals. She has a soft corner for birds. Her love for the environment is strongly reflected in her book. Her desire is for people to connect to their true self, their inner child. She believes that this is best done by connecting with nature because humans are made up of the elements of Mother Earth. She is also passionate about environmental justice, wildlife conservation and animal welfare.

Self-empowerment cannot be achieved holistically, separate from the environment in which we live. This is Meera's take on personal growth. As she puts it – *When Mother Earth thrives, we thrive!*

You can connect with Meera on these platforms:

YouTube -
https://www.youtube.com/channel/UCeMgayabCdcM8YxSLtdfTVQ
Twitter - https://twitter.com/MJhogasundram
Instagram - https://www.instagram.com/meera_author_coach/
Website - https://meerajhogasundram.com
Facebook Page - https://www.facebook.com/MeeraJhogasundram
Facebook - https://www.facebook.com/jhogasundram
TikTok – https://www.tiktok.com/@meera_jhogasundram
Pinterest - https://www.pinterest.ch/MeeraJhogasundram/_created/
LinkedIn - https://www.linkedin.com/in/meerajhogasundram/

WHAT DO YOU THINK OF *YOU ARE THE KEY?*

First and foremost, thank you for purchasing my book, *You are the key.* Given your numerous options, you chose this book. I am grateful for your choice and support.

If you enjoyed this book and gained knowledge and value that you can use for your own journey in empowerment, I humbly request you to spare 5 minutes of your time to post a review about *You are the key* at Amazon.

Your support and feedback is invaluable for the content of my forthcoming books and projects. It will help me cater to your requirements even better in future.

Living your best life requires you to fully realise your potential and worth. It requires you to unconditionally accept and love yourself. Every positive change that you desire in your life begins with you. Make the choice to motivate, inspire and empower yourself so that you will live your dream.

Remember...it's up to you!

Wishing you the very best in all your endeavours,

Meera Jhogasundram

Your Free Gift

Thank you for purchasing my book!
I value each and every one of my readers.
As a gesture of gratitude, I'm offering a free digital product exclusively
for you, my readers.

"How to deal with toxic people – 3 effective ways!!!"

To learn more, go to the link below and get immediate access:

https://www.subscribepage.com/youarethekey